PRAISE FOR *FATHERLESS GENERATION*

John Sowers is the "voice crying in ... turn our faces toward the devastation ... beautifully written book is not a wringing of the hands, but a p... ful and strategic call to action.

William Paul Young, author of *The Shack*

Fatherless Generation illuminates the longing and hurt that fuel the decisions of a generation seeking acceptance, hope, assurance, and truth. With prose that is personal, direct, and eloquent, *Fatherless Generation* is emotionally charged and boldly honest, and it holds the key to real healing for the reader, whether they are fatherless or love someone who is.

Dan Merchant, writer/director of
Lord, Save Us from Your Followers

John Sowers has tapped into the powerful theme of *belonging* and accurately describes the fatherless generation that is longing for it. Through John's personal story, he exposes the shame of millions growing up without fathers and points the reader in the direction of hope and compassionate action. This is a powerful book.

Dr. Tom Phillips, vice president
of the Billy Graham Evangelistic Association

I believe that the church can solve the problem of fatherlessness. And this book is our call. It is our call to something that the biblical writer James calls "true religion," our call to do something that matters deeply to the heart of God.

Gabe Lyons, author of *The Next Christians*
and coauthor of *UnChristian*

FATHERLESS GENERATION

REDEEMING THE STORY

JOHN SOWERS

 ZONDERVAN®

ZONDERVAN

Fatherless Generation
Copyright © 2010 by John A. Sowers

This title is also available as a Zondervan ebook.

This title is also available in a Zondervan audio edition.

Requests for information should be addressed to:
Zondervan, 3900 *Sparks Dr. SE, Grand Rapids, Michigan 49546*

Library of Congress Cataloging-in-Publication Data

Sowers, John, 1974-
    Fatherless generation : redeeming the story / John Sowers.
        p. cm.
    ISBN 978-0-310-32860-5
    1. God (Christianity)—Fatherhood. 2. Paternal deprivation—Religious aspects—
Christianity. 3. Absentee fathers. I. Title.
BT153.F3S63 2010
    248.8'421—dc22   2010010860

Cover design: Rob Monacelli
Interior design: Matthew VanZomeren

Printed in the United States of America

16 17 18 19 20 21 22 23 24 25 26 27 /DCI/ 22 21 20 19 18 17 16 15 14 13 12 11 10 9 8 7

For Karilyn,
the Rose of My Heart

CONTENTS

FOREWORD BY DONALD MILLER

JOHN SOWERS IS LIVING PROOF that God can take fatherless boys and turn them into men of integrity and excellence, men who lead movements and love their wives, and even men who write books.

I met John a few years ago through a friend, and after discovering he'd written his doctoral dissertation on the crisis of fatherlessness, we asked him to join our board of directors at *The Mentoring Project*. Soon after that, we realized John was the man who was supposed to lead our little movement, so we asked him to come on as our president. John said yes, and about a week later stripped me of all my power, save talking very nicely about *The Mentoring Project*, raising money for the organization, and mentoring a kid. Seriously, I don't even get to choose what kind of coffee we serve in the office. More proof, perhaps, that he is a wise and brilliant leader.

Since we hired John, he has become my friend. I am very proud of him, and he is very proud of me. Fatherless men need friends who are proud of them. It feeds our souls to have friends who are proud of us. John can write a book and lead an organization, but in the end, he's a fatherless kid looking for somebody to be proud of him. I know because that's exactly who I am too. And if you're reading this book, maybe that's who you are as well.

John and I have a similar story. When we were kids, men from our church took us under their wings and taught us how to be men.

These men weren't our fathers, but they were men provided by God, and evidence that God has a heart for fatherless kids. Without these men, I'd most likely be in prison. John may have fared better, but it's statistically doubtful.

I started *The Mentoring Project* years ago, but I soon realized it was John's vision too. As we compared notes, I knew God had put the exact same idea on our hearts, the idea that men in churches all over the country could mentor fatherless boys and help solve this crisis of fatherlessness. When boys have positive male role models, they are less likely to get in trouble. Around *The Mentoring Project* office, we believe we can actually shut down some prisons in our country by modeling positive character for an abandoned generation.

These days, John and I have realized the vision wasn't ours; it was God's. And God is putting the same vision in the hearts of thousands of men all over America. If that vision rings true with you, please join our movement.

Read this book, and then tell your friends about it. Find out what we are doing at *The Mentoring Project*. Help us turn the heart of the church to the fatherless.

Donald Miller

AUTHOR'S NOTE

THIS BOOK WAS BORN in the trenches of my own journey and in the heart of my generation. Growing up without a father around deeply affected me, although I didn't really understand this until I was in my midtwenties. When I did, I woke up to the millions of young people around me who were struggling with this same issue: *fatherlessness.*

At the same time that I began dealing with my own issues of fatherlessness, I started asking questions: What does it mean for a generation to grow up without Dad? What happens when Dad walks out the door of your life, never to return? What happens when our givers of life give us a lifetime of tears?

On January 10, 2008, I wrote a blog called "Tell Your Story."* It reads:

> There is something beautiful and powerful about a story. Each of us has a story filled with unique experiences of brokenness, betrayal, bitterness. Experiences of elation, gratitude, laughter, and joy. These experiences shape our stories and define our lives....
>
> I think it's a common reality for most of us to be quiet about our fatherlessness. Maybe because being fatherless makes us feel ashamed, like black sheep that everyone makes fun of, or picks at,

---

* Visit *www.myspace.com/thefatherlessgeneration.*

11

or ignores altogether. Maybe fatherlessness makes us feel like less of a person. Maybe it makes us angry, sending us flying off into fits of rage. Maybe we've swallowed it for so long trying to convince ourselves it never happened. Or maybe just thinking about it hurts too much.

But there is something healing in sharing our stories.

A couple of years ago, I went to New Orleans immediately after Katrina. We were sent to sit with people in the ashes of a broken city. While there, I scrambled and searched and racked my brain thinking about what I could say. What words could I bring that meant anything to someone who lost everything?

The longer I sat with those broken people, the more I realized that I had nothing to give. No eloquent words or prerehearsed formulas. The only thing I could offer was silence. And when I offered this gift, first one, then two, then dozens of people began opening up and sharing their stories. I began realizing that there was something healing in the silence. And in the sharing.

Hope seemed to emerge and rise from the despair. Hope wasn't found in anything I was saying. Hope was found in the sharing.

The sharing meant that someone cared enough to listen. It meant that the storyteller was a valid person. It meant that they were not alone. It meant that their story mattered. And it meant that they mattered.

This page exists to tell you that you are not alone and that your story matters. And that you matter. It is my hope that this will be a safe place for you to share your story. Maybe somehow you will find hope in doing so. Maybe redemption really is stories to tell.

After I posted this entry, I had no idea what was about to happen. In the first few months, I received thousands of responses from people all over the world—people connecting to the page and sharing their stories, their experiences with fatherlessness. I was bombarded with comments and emails and friend requests. Some were hopeful; others were not. Some were angry; others were grateful.

As I read these entries, I realized I was tapping into a larger story. A story defining the way we think, the way we feel, the way we relate, and the way we live and love. A story affecting the lives of a generation.

This book is my response to that story.

Maybe this book will be a voice for you, helping you articulate your own story. Maybe it will make you more aware of those around you—a generation of fatherless people who are crying out for help. I hope it will stir you and move you to action.

The book is written in two distinct parts. The first part is a call to listen, to connect with the story. My hope is that you will *feel* the emotion—the rejection, the raw anger, and the haunting shame, the themes so deeply woven into this story. The second part is a call to movement, to *advocate* and to *act* on behalf of the fatherless. It shines light on people who are redeeming this story. May their heroic and catalytic action spark a movement across our country.

Even though this book is written from my limited perspective—which is masculine and unique to my experience—this story is bigger than gender, age, or race. I didn't write it to put blame on absent fathers or to create a generation of proud victims. And the title, *Fatherless Generation*, is a bit of a misnomer. As one blogger commented, "This generation has a Father—he just hasn't been properly introduced yet."

PART ONE

FATHERLESS GENERATION

CHAPTER 1

SOMEWHERE I BELONG

I wanna find something I've wanted all along
Somewhere I belong, somewhere I belong
from the song "Somewhere I Belong," by Linkin Park

THE EARLIEST MEMORIES OF MY FATHER are the few times he came to visit us during the Christmas season. About once a year, he would drive up from Austin to Little Rock for the weekend. My brother and I usually stayed with him at the Motel 6. Back then, Motel 6 had the big mechanical beds that, for only a quarter, would shake and make a low humming noise. Sleeping on them was like riding a giant, lumbering submarine.

My father usually smelled like an odd mixture of Old Spice and musky sweat. And for most of my childhood, I just thought that was how a man was supposed to smell. Sometimes he let me "drive" his burgundy Monte Carlo, which consisted of sitting in his lap and playing with the dark hair on his arms.

My brother Bill and I always ended up fighting for his attention. To us, his attention was a prize to be won. To be earned. It was as if we had one weekend to catch up on an entire year of absence. One chance to have him notice us, look at us, be proud of us, and love us. One brief moment to shine for this elusive man we called "Dad."

I remember the park swings. Swinging beside him, trying to keep up, to go as high as him. I wanted him to be close to him, to make him proud. My brother and I took our Polaroid camera with us to the park to capture these moments. I hoarded these pictures and placed them in a big red album, poring over them for countless hours.

These pictures represented seismic moments of *acceptance*. Moments of joy and belonging. Moments of life as it was supposed to be. Dad was here with us, with me, and everything was all right because of it.

Secretly, I hoped he might stay around this time. Just maybe. If we pleased him enough and were good enough, he just might stay. He might stay home with us, where he belonged. So I continued to live my little fantasy until it was time for his inevitable departure.

I remember once grabbing his ankles — hanging on for dear life — as he walked out the front door, dragging me as I pleaded with him to stay. I was fighting for his affection, literally. But it didn't work. It never worked.

Each time he left, my heart would break and I would die again.

Somewhere along the way, I grew callous. As his visits grew more infrequent, the promise of Dad became remote. He became a faceless voice on the phone. A signature on a birthday card. A fading image on an old, yellow Polaroid.

Eventually I let go of the hope that he would ever stay. It simply hurt too much to hope. So I buried it like some lost and forgotten treasure. I hid away my red picture album under piles of books and shoeboxes full of baseball cards, swearing to never look at it again. As the years passed, I began to accept the reality that he wasn't coming back. And nothing I could do would ever change that. So I stopped performing, stopped caring.

THE FATHERLESS STORY

Rejection is the defining characteristic of the fatherless generation.

In the United States alone, just over 33 percent of youth — over 25 million kids — are fatherless and searching for Dad.[1] They are searching for his love and acceptance. But Dad is nowhere to be found. He has run off to Vegas with a younger woman. He is lost in an alcoholic fog. He is sitting in a jail cell in Memphis. He is gone.

Fatherlessness creates an appetite in the soul that demands fulfillment.

> Fatherlessness creates an appetite in the soul that demands fulfillment.

Over time, the unmet needs created by Dad's absence turn into something that author Robert McGee calls "father hunger." And in America alone, millions are starving to death. McGee states, "People who grow up starved for a father's love become victims of an anonymous mugger or a faceless cancer."[2]

To live with father hunger is to live with the sadness of what will never be. Perhaps the worst thing about this rejection is living with the knowledge that someone has *chosen* to turn his back on you. Someone has chosen to leave you. Someone has determined your value and decided you are not worth having around — or that he would be better off someplace else, without you.

I first met Shay when she posted a response on my "Tell Your Story" blog. Even though she was only five when her father moved out, she was convinced it was her fault that he left. She writes:

When I was five years old, my father left. I didn't understand what was happening. I can remember the day so well. My father gathered his things and walked outside to get into a cab. I was standing there confused, and he gave me a kiss and said that he loved me and he'd see me soon. It's been more than thirteen years, and I still don't know my father or really care to know him. The hardest part about growing up without him was feeling like it was somehow my fault. I felt like he hated me or didn't ever really love me at all.*

Another fatherless blogger, Aron, wrestles with his father's rejection. His dad was his best friend. Now he wonders if that rejection is contagious. He shares:

Growing up, I was used to having my dad around. He was always there for me. He got me into the things I love today, like football and video games. He was my hero. When I was nine, my dad left my family. Not having any explanation for why my daddy left me had a great impact on me during my preteen years. The only reason I thought he left me was because he didn't love me. This caused me to run from family, friends, and God. I mean, if my own father couldn't love me, how could anyone else?*

When Dad leaves, something dies.

PROPHETS OF OUR CULTURE

Pop culture captures the dying voice of this generation. In it, we hear poets and prophets crying out for hope in the midst of ruin. Pop culture is a warped mirror of our lives. And if we can just pause to listen, we hear a song of despair rising from the ashes.

In his song "Father of Mine," Art Alexakis, lead singer of the rock band Everclear remembers, "My dad he gave me a name; then

---

* Visit *www.myspace.com/thefatherlessgeneration*, "Tell Your Story."

he walked away."[3] In an interview for this book, Art shared with me that his father abandoned his family when he was young, walking out on him and his brother and three sisters. Because of financial problems, his mom relocated to the housing projects in Los Angeles, where Art was introduced to the drug culture. His brother, George, overdosed on heroin when Art was twelve, and that same year Art's girlfriend committed suicide. Not long after, Art tried to kill himself by filling his pockets with weights and jumping off the Santa Monica pier. This is what Art said about the song "Father of Mine":

> Pop culture is a warped mirror of our lives. And if we can just pause to listen, we hear a song of despair rising from the ashes.

> The song is really personal. I grew up with a single mom, and we lived in the projects. So the song is true story—and a universal theme. A lot of us can relate to the pain and shame that comes from being fatherless. We have damage and baggage. I think it's our job to break the cycle, to pass on less damage and baggage to the next generation, to our sons and daughters. That is what I tell people from the stage when I talk about "Father of Mine."

In their song "Hey Dad," the pop-punk band Good Charlotte asks, "Do you remember me, the son that you conceived?"[4] Singer Alecia Beth Moore, better known as P!nk, in her song "Family Portrait" cries out, "Daddy don't leave, don't leave us here alone."[5] In an interview with *Entertainment Weekly*, P!nk talks about her song:

> I wanted to talk about [my life], and there it is. But every interview is like, "You're a very tormented child, aren't you? How was your childhood?" ... So that was a song I was a little paranoid about. That's why the video was the way it was. It was a little girl

singing instead of me, because it's too much for me. That little girl was me.*

Why do records like these sell millions of copies every year? Why are the live shows sold out night after night? Why do thousands of fans religiously flock to these singers and follow their every move on Twitter and Facebook?

This is more than loud music. More than mosh pits and star worship. More than flashing lights and smoke machines. Something deeper is going on here. A soulful identification is taking place, even if most of the listeners cannot articulate it. It is raw emotion played out loud.

> We are a generation that desperately wants to be found, a generation that desperately wants to be home.

Pain, rage, and despair individually felt and corporately experienced.

These are the anthems of the fatherless generation.

These are our songs. These are sacred blues, formed in the emotional poverty of a generation. Sung by men and women speaking for the masses. Sung from the guts of their own experience.

We are a rejected generation, left behind to pick up the fragile pieces of our broken existence. Confused, we grope in the dark for meaning, purpose, and hope. Alone, we hide behind machine and computer screen, projecting voiceless signals out into the oblivion. We grasp for anything that feels like acceptance but are too afraid to open our hearts and embrace it for it ourselves.

We are a generation displaced. A refugee generation, shuffling from one shelter to the next in search of belonging. We are a genera-

---

* Chris Willman, " 'Try' a Little Tenderness," *Entertainment Weekly*, *http://www .ew.com/ew/article/0,,490980.html*.

tion that desperately wants to be found, a generation that desperately wants to be home.

A couple of years ago, I ran into actor Will Ferrell outside the *Saturday Night Live* studio in New York. At the time, I was working on my doctoral dissertation and was using references to his movie *Elf* in my introduction. After my friend unceremoniously hailed him over, I decided to say something to him about his movie and my paper. Our conversation went something like this:

Me: "Hey, man, I'm a really big *Elf* fan."

Will: "Oh yeah?"

Me: "Yeah. And actually I'm using it in the introduction to my doctoral dissertation."

Will: "Really?"

Me: "Yeah, the story of Elf is the story of our generation. Like Buddy, our generation is furiously searching for Dad. We go to great lengths to find him and earn his acceptance. But unfortunately, most of the time, Dad does not want to be found."

Will: "Hmm." (Shrugs his shoulders and walks away.)

We are a generation furiously searching for Dad, but Dad is nowhere to be found. For over 25 million of us, he has walked out the doors of our lives, never to return home. Fatherlessness has now become the cultural norm. This story is being written into the lives of my generation. A story that can be heard in our songs, seen in our movies, read in our blogs. A story of grief and pain, of loneliness and rejection.

A story that desperately needs to be heard.

CHAPTER 2

HAUNTED HOUSES

Left ...
To face death and life alone,
Haunted by the face that was once one of our own.
Now, a disembodied cry hangs stranded,
Afloat on the howling wind —
No anchor to plant us amidst our growing strife,
No touch to give us feeling,
No breath to give us life.

John Sowers

DAD AND I KEPT IN TOUCH a couple of times a year. I continued making
my obligatory visits to Austin every summer. But those visits were
awkward. It was like trying to catch up with someone you never
knew in the first place. My entire world was in Little Rock. My best
friends, my Little League baseball team, my neighborhood pool, and
my Putt-Putt golf course where I played video games every Saturday.
How do you share that with someone in a week?

Although I didn't see him much, I never hated my dad or carried
any hostility toward him. I wasn't bitter or angry, and I always liked

being around him. But seeing my father only once a year formed a callousness in me. His ongoing absence made him a nonentity. As I grew up, I turned inward, often carrying on long and detailed conversations with myself. My mom told me it was OK to talk to myself, as long as my self didn't talk back. Sometimes I got so lost in my own world that I forgot where I was and would mumble to myself in public. I think that when you feel alone, any sound is comforting, even if it's your own voice.

My early days at school were spent daydreaming. Teachers faded as I locked in on a sheet of paper that became my magic canvas—a canvas for creating new characters for my next imaginary adventure. I filled up notebooks with drawings of knights, dragons, and ninjas. Cloaking myself in a fantasy world, I spent hours locked away inside my own safe little world.

But from time to time I still thought of my dad.

At T-ball games I secretly wished he would show up and be proud. I wanted him to see me in my blue Coyotes uniform. I dreamed of him watching me hit the ball or turn a double play. But he missed my first game—and every game after that. He missed my riding a bike for the first time when I was five. He missed my splitting my head open on a brick and needing stitches. He missed my singing "Do-Re-Mi" in the school play. He missed the first bass I caught in Lake Conway. He missed the book on planets that I wrote, illustrated, and published in the Terry Elementary School library. He missed my childhood altogether.

LIFE WITH THE GHOST

Although Dad may be absent, the ghost of his influence faithfully remains. Some seek to answer the absence by performing. "Dad is watching us," we think, "and we must make him proud." So we live our lives trying to prove ourselves to him. We chase after the corporate executive position. Push ourselves to be a better golfer. Drive the Jaguar. Live in the suburban sprawl. We strain toward the more and the bigger. We will measure up, even if it kills us. We still think about Dad at major life intersections or after another accomplishment. We want his validation in those moments. We look to him in his presence and his absence, wondering what would please him, what would make him proud.

> Although Dad may be absent, the ghost of his influence remains.

Or we are hell-bent on never making him proud. We swear to be nothing like him. Dad becomes our doppelgänger, a dark shadow looming in the background. We reject whatever vision we think he had for our lives, carpet bombing his memory with hate and indifference. Trying to forget him altogether.

Dad is gone. And in our anger, we convince ourselves that we will never live for his ghost. Yet, in spite of our best efforts, we are driven by our rejection, just as those who are driven to please him. The ghost reminds us who *not* to be, which defines the framework of who we *are* to be. Our identity is shaped by our defiance. In the song "Take a Picture," Richard Patrick of the band Filter screams at his ghost, "Hey, Dad, what do you think about your son now?"[6]

Each of us has this visceral longing, a primal urge to be accepted by our father and to make him proud. This urge is something like hunger or the need for sleep — it stays with us our entire lives. When Dad is not around, this urge becomes a haunting. The ghost usually takes on the form of a question. We may bring our question to other men, or every man we meet. We may bring our question to the world of women. We may bring our question to the mirror and remain haunted by its booming silence. We wonder, "Do you see me? Will you validate me?" All the while, the question grows louder in our hearts. Bestselling author Seth Godin writes on his blog, " 'Notice me.' If the new Web has a mantra, that's it. So much time and effort is now put into finding followers, accumulating comments, and generating controversy—all so that people will notice you. People say and do things that don't benefit them, just because they're hooked on attention."[7]

I looked to appease the ghost in other male relationships. Unknowingly, I brought my question to anyone who would hear it. Anyone who might notice me. Anyone who could validate my existence.

One of those guys was my Kenpo Karate instructor named Keith. I started taking karate with Keith when I was twelve. Like just about every other boy who ever lived, I secretly wanted to be a ninja. Keith is an amazing martial artist and person. He was recently inducted into the Karate Hall of Fame alongside Bruce Lee and Chuck Norris. Keith could kick his way through a fireplace mantel. He could also jump up and kick a ceiling fan, which can be incredibly handy at times. Keith had a big, bushy moustache when they were cool, like Tom Selleck's.

During class we practiced combinations and forms. Sometimes we would free spar. We would gear up with mouthpieces and pads on our hands, feet, and shins and split into two lines facing each other. We would then fight everyone in the class. On Fridays, we trained with weapons. I got pretty good with a bo staff. Usually after class we spontaneously wrestled, and I'd inevitably end up on my head as Keith held me upside down by my ankles.

For several years, Keith, his wife Karla, and I drove all over the South fighting at karate tournaments. We piled into his brown Isuzu Trooper and drove around Arkansas, Tennessee, Mississippi, Louisiana, Texas, and little towns all around this land. Right before we went into each tournament, Keith put "Eye of the Tiger" into the cassette player to get us ready for battle. I remember sitting in that truck, being proud of Keith and proud that I was about to go to war with him. The tournament was usually held in a high school gymnasium, with the "rings" being taped off by squares on the dusty wooden floor. After I finished my weapon and kata forms and my fighting rounds, I would proudly watch Keith disassemble every black belt in the region. And he did. Keith destroyed people.

In a lot of ways, Keith was like a father to me. We didn't have a lot of long talks. We did talk about being grateful and respectful, but being around Keith was more about discovery. And permission. Keith was someone I could be proud of. Someone I could look to and know I was normal. That it was normal to wrestle, to be honorable, and to fight and be wild at times.

But a lot of us are not as fortunate. There are simply not enough Keiths to go around. The longer we live with our doubts, the more vulnerable we become to believing the lies of the ghosts. And the longer we live with the ghost, the easier it becomes to sink into despair. We begin to see the world with a skewed perspective.

SHAME: RESIDUE FROM THE GHOST

One way that the fatherless ghost takes root in our souls is through shame. Shame is our pervasive sense of embarrassment. To live in shame is to live disgraced. It's the compelling and constant need to apologize for everything, including ourselves. Our entire life may feel like one big apology. We may walk around, hanging our head, constantly feeling like a huge disappointment to everyone. Many of the fatherless are ashamed of themselves, ashamed of the way they feel, ashamed of the wounds they carry.

In his bestselling book *Iron John*, poet and author Robert Bly writes, "Shame, it is said, is the sense that you are an utterly inadequate person on this planet and nothing can be done about it.... To be without a supportive father is for a man, an alternative phrase for 'to be in shame.'"[8] Conflicted, we bring this shame-induced inadequacy into everything we do — the relationships we have, the way we think, live, and believe. We bring our inadequacy to the workplace, with something to prove, and we either quit or become workaholics. We bring our inadequacy to our peers and become people pleasers or rebels. We bring our inadequacy to a relationship, and when it doesn't answer the question, we blame, move on, or wallow in despair. We face our inadequacy and become victims or performers. We try to escape the inadequacy and become irresponsible or addicted. We project our inadequacy onto God and feel that God is ashamed of us and that we must perform flawlessly to earn and keep his approval.

> One way that the fatherless ghost takes root in our souls is through shame.

Growing up, I never felt it was good enough to be me. I felt I had to compete for the affection and attention I so desperately needed. But no matter how much I accomplished, I still felt incomplete, broken. I hated the shame I carried inside and desperately tried to forget it.

Some of the obvious signs of fatherless shame are slumping shoulders, heads hung low, and an aversion to eye contact. The person who lives in shame feels unworthy to look at anyone directly. So he hunkers down, mumbling and shuffling along. He tries to go by unnoticed, not wanting to blow his cover. When his cover is finally blown, his shame and brokenness surfaces. He may purposely sabotage himself at work or school. He may lash out at his peers or cry uncontrollably over their rejection. But most of the time, he chooses to remain passive, fearing rejection. He would rather just slide by.

In *Man Enough*, Frank Pittman states, "Men without models don't know what is behind their shame, loneliness, and despair, their desperate search for love, for affirmation, and for structure, their frantic tendency to compete over just about anything with just about anybody."[9] Fatherless boys don't boast about their father's occupation at show-and-tell. They are the last to brag in the school lunchroom about whose dad is the biggest and baddest. They cannot enter these conversations with boyish pride. A fatherless boy doesn't join the "dad" conversation at all. He has to duck. He turns away, hoping he will not be called on. *"Hey, what about your dad? How tough is he? What does he do?"*

The fatherless boy lives with the nagging accusation that he will never be adequate, never measure up, never really be a man. For the young man who lives in shame, manhood seems just out of reach — like it belongs to an aloof group of faceless men who live somewhere "over there." One blogger, Jasper411, writes, "When I was a kid, I always felt the other boys had some access to secret male knowledge that I didn't have. This included such important life skills as catching a ball, tying a tie, picking up girls, etc.... I felt like not having a father, I didn't know what 'masculine' meant."*

Some young boys are so crippled by this shame-induced inadequacy that they never embrace responsibility, never maturing into

---

* Visit *www.askmetafilter.com*, "Fatherless" (July 18, 2006), *http://ask.metafilter .com/42442/Fatherless*.

adults. The ghost reminds them of the reality that no one is there for them, that no one "has their back." Debilitated by their inadequacy, they live in a continual state of apathy. "Everyone has given up on me," they think, "so why should I care about anything? Why should I even try?" Stuck in life, they hold no other motivation beyond playing video games, watching sports, and hanging out. Some drop out of school or bounce from job to job or relationship to relationship. It is a rootless life, without purpose and vision for the future. They may even father a child and then abandon her, thus repeating the cycle of fatherlessness.

Fatherless girls struggle with shame as well. Girls mourn the missed opportunities to stand on the living room table and spin their twirling dresses for Dad. They dream of being beautiful, adored, noticed, of shining for him and captivating his attention. They wonder if they are even worth noticing at all. Another blogger, Beth, made this comment:

> I used to be Daddy's princess. I woke up early and was informed by my dad that he was leaving. He spoke about how it was going to be all right. But the tearstains on my mom's face proved him wrong. I didn't know what to think or what to say. All that came to mind was "OK," and that is exactly what I said. I guess I was trying to convince myself that everything *was* OK. It wasn't, and before I knew it, he had left.
>
> We all handled it differently. My older brother chased Dad's car. My mother cried and basically stopped functioning for months.... And I just kind of held it in. Seven years later, I still, to this day, hold it in.... I have issues with my self-esteem. And find it hard to trust people. I hope that one day, the wounds I have inside will heal.*

---

* Visit *www.myspace.com/thefatherlessgeneration*, "Tell Your Story."

Chained to the past, the fatherless generation lives a haunted existence. Their souls are like haunted houses. The ghost is a daily reminder of inadequacy and shame. They will live with the pressure to prove themselves to Dad, or prove that they never needed him anyway. The weight of it all can be crippling. But usually, it's a weight that can't be felt anymore. Like a damp wool coat three sizes too big, it engulfs them, hanging several inches past their hands, dragging on the ground. Sometimes they can feel it and wish it would go away. But it remains with them all the same.

CHAPTER 3

MIDNIGHT SONS AND DAUGHTERS

Abed: Really great to have somebody to watch stuff with. My dad never wanted to watch anything. So I was kinda raised by TV.

Jeff: TV's the best dad there is. TV never came home drunk. TV never forgot me at the zoo. TV never abused and insulted me.

from the TV show Community—
a conversation between Abed and Jeff

I RECENTLY PICKED UP A BOOK by bestselling author Augusten Burroughs titled *A Wolf at the Table: A Memoir of My Father*. Augusten describes growing up with his distant father. He tried crawling into his father's lap repeatedly, only to be pushed away time and time again. Augusten even kept a written scorecard of these "attempts," recording his father's constant denials.

One day, after what seemed to be an endless sea of failed attempts, young Augusten decided to make a "father body." Sneaking a plaid shirt from the bathroom closet and a pair of slacks from his father's dresser, he began to create his mannequin. He stuffed the clothes with towels and pillows, shaping them into the form of arms, legs, and a torso.

Then, carefully and secretly, he laid his creation in his bed. At night, Augusten would lie next to his father body, pretending to be loved and held. Every morning, he disassembled the body and safely stored it away. He writes:

> I crawled into bed beside the body, turned on my side, and curled against it.
>
> A trace, a mere whiff of my father's cologne clung to the shirt's fibers when I pressed my face against its chest. It was an acceptable substitute.
>
> Drowsiness overtook me like a drug. The father body had an intoxicating effect on me, and if I had spoken, my words would have been slurred. . . .
>
> Never again would I attempt to snuggle up with my father.
>
> Now when I needed him, I would go to my room and assemble the body, place it on the bed, and hug it.[10]

What drives someone to make a father body to sleep with at night? As strange as it sounds, I know that Augusten's experience isn't unusual. Children like Augusten are everywhere, even though they are not broadcasting it in bestselling books.

• • •

My wife and I have known our friend Angie for about ten years. She has this easy grace about her that draws people in. It seems like people are always hovering around her in little packs, as if at any moment she might hand out warm chocolate chip cookies.

We've known and watched Angie's story develop for a number of years. When she was a little girl, her dad left home and moved to another country. He's now a crop duster pilot living thousands of miles away from their hometown of Searcy, Arkansas. And when Angie found out I was writing about fatherlessness, she gave me a letter about her early memories of her father. Here are some excerpts:

> My mom and dad divorced when I was three, so my early memories of Dad are few and far between. Some of those memories are nonexistent. Maybe that is a gift. I do have one memory as a little girl, probably about two years old, where I am dancing my heart out to the radio, while Dad is looking on and smiling and laughing and thinking I am so cute. He thought it was so funny that I would stand there in my diaper on that shag carpet and wiggle to the beat. Even then, I was trying to get his attention. I can't count how many times I have relived that memory. It was a moment full of hope for both of us. But I've often wondered where it all went wrong. Was the 'Dad gene' missing? Was it Vietnam? Was it the fact that his dad died when he was a boy? Was it Mom? Was it me?
>
> He moved out of the country about twelve years ago and has only been back two or three times since. I still hear from him occasionally when he leaves a message on my cell phone. It makes me sad when I hear his voice. It is riddled with guilt. I always save his messages, although I don't know why. I cherish them, just like I cherish the sporadic visits of the past. Each time, I feel like it may be the last time I hear from him, and I don't know how I will feel when he dies. I may regret not making more of an effort to contact him and develop a relationship with him. I know my lack of emotion for him bothers me, and I want that to change. I do feel like I love him in some strange way. But how can you love someone you don't know? Can you love the idea of someone? Can you love someone out of pity?

One word that keeps jumping out at me through stories like Augusten's and Angie's is *proximity*. Proximity is our constant urge to be close to Dad, to touch his beard and to hold his attention. It is a primal desire that we never outgrow. More than the doing and performing, we long to be near him. And when Dad is near, we cling to these moments of hope. Moments that become indelibly engraved in our memory, pressed down as weight in our souls.

> Over time, the shame, hopelessness, and despair that we feel may turn into something darker, something destructive.

The power of proximity can best be seen through its absence. Maybe it is best illustrated by observing those who have lost it, those who are crying out the loudest for their dads. Life feels like a recurring funeral procession. Even though Dad is gone, we live in a state of denial, hoping he will come back. Hoping he will rise from the dead. But our deep sense of loss is not the end of the story. Over time, the shame, hopelessness, and despair that we feel may turn into something darker, something destructive.

THE FALLOUT

A host of studies have shown that this fatherless-driven destruction has taken America hostage. The fatherless generation is accountable for most of the serious social problems we face today. According to various sources, children from fatherless homes account for

63 percent of youth suicides

71 percent of pregnant teenagers

90 percent of all homeless and runaway children

70 percent of juveniles in state-operated institutions

85 percent of all youth who exhibit behavior disorders

80 percent of rapists motivated with displaced anger

71 percent of all high school dropouts

75 percent of all adolescents in chemical abuse centers

85 percent of all youths sitting in prison.[11]

What's more, children from fatherless homes are nearly twice as likely to struggle with hyperactivity, conduct, and emotional disorders and have a social impairment. They are nearly three times as likely to be struggling in school or to have repeated a grade. They are five times more likely to be poor, thirty-three times more likely to be seriously abused (requiring medical attention), and seventy-three times more likely to be killed.[12]

Fight Club, a movie based on the popular book by Chuck Palahniuk, dropped like a hammer on the American male psyche, becoming an instant cult classic. The movie chronicles the life of Tyler Durden and his followers—a tribe of violent men searching for meaning in the bloody world of underground fighting. The men join Tyler's tribe to test themselves and to find something more than their materialistic, shallow existences.

At first glance, it doesn't seem to make sense. Why would these guys want to pound each other into a bloody mess? What makes them enjoy being a part of that? But Fight Club is much more than the fighting. There are rules and mutual respect. There are sacred lines not to be crossed. Fight Club is an honor code, a way of life, a rite of passage for the men.

Tyler is deeply conflicted, living a split personality. In the real world, he is a cubicle-dwelling wimp. But in his mind, he is an outlaw and a fighter. The wimp is attracted to the danger of the outlaw. At the same time, the outlaw is tormented, full of questions, nihilism, and cynicism. As the story unfolds, his two identities merge. The wimp slowly becomes the outlaw. Eventually, Tyler and his followers become consumed with megalomania, violence, and anarchy.

But the underlying question that *Fight Club* is found in a conversation that macho Tyler has with the narrator, his alter ego. The narrator asks, "If you could fight anyone, who would you fight?"

Tyler responds, "I'd fight my dad."

The narrator says, "I didn't know my dad. Well, I knew him, but he left when I was like six years old, married this other woman, and had a lotta kids. He like did this every six years — goes to a new city and starts a new family."

Tyler says, "My dad never went to college, so it was real important that I go. So I graduate. I call him up long distance and said, 'Dad, now what?' He says, 'Get a job' — maybe I should now I'm twenty-five. Make my yearly call again and said, 'Dad, now what?' He says, 'I don't know. Get married.'... We're a generation of men raised by women, and I'm wondering if another woman is really the answer we need."[13]

My reference here to *Fight Club* is not an endorsement for the movie. But its disturbing content does illuminate the darkness engulfing the fatherless generation. Tyler looks to his absent father for validation. At the same time, he despises his father and wants to fight him (and every other living person, for that matter). The question that *Fight Club* voices for a generation must be heard: Where do the fatherless turn to find what they are so desperately looking for? Left without an answer, they inevitably consume and destroy themselves, each other, and their communities.

> Where do the fatherless turn to find what they are so desperately looking for?

Stockholm syndrome is a term used to describe the psychological phenomenon where captives desire the approval of their captors. It is why some hostages love terrorists, why some sane people follow psychopaths like Tyler Durden. It is why—to a lesser degree—we compromise ourselves without realizing we are really seeking acceptance. Those held captive by the father's ghost compromise themselves in a desperate search for belonging.

The fatherless generation is suffering from Stockholm syndrome.

Shelly, a fatherless teenager who connected with me on MySpace, talks about her ongoing cycle of self-destructive behavior. Over a short period of time, her anger, frustration, and depression isolated her from family and friends and led her into habitual self-injury that she describes as "comforting." She writes:

> Three days before my twelfth birthday, my father told us that he wanted a divorce. He said he didn't love my mom anymore and he was leaving. That was it. No warning. Nothing. I was so frustrated. I grew bitter, angry, depressed. The rest of the family became the same way, and we took out our frustrations on each other. To say that we fell into decay would be an understatement.... Those around me said I looked like a living skull. I had no problems hurting myself or striking my head against the wall. The pain was comforting. The kids at school didn't know what to do with me— the skull. They left me alone.*

The generational loss of father proximity is devastating. Fatherless boys and girls are swallowing heaping doses of shame, bitterness, and anger and are growing sick as a result. Author and researcher David Blankenhorn states:

> Fatherlessness is the most harmful demographic trend of this generation. It is the leading cause of declining child well-being in our society. It is also the engine driving our most urgent social problems, from crime to adolescent pregnancy to child sexual abuse to domestic violence against women. Yet, despite its scale and social

---

* Visit *www.myspace.com/thefatherlessgeneration*, "Tell Your Story."

consequences, fatherlessness is a problem that is frequently ignored or denied.[14]

In 1965, Senator Daniel Patrick Moynihan called attention to the dangers of boys growing up without their fathers, given the increasing trend toward a fatherless society. Moynihan understood that fatherlessness affects more than just single mothers and fatherless children; he warned that unless something drastically changed, our nation itself would descend into crime, violence, and anarchy. He said, "A community that allows large numbers of young men to grow up in broken families, dominated by women, never acquiring any stable relationship with male authority, never acquiring any rational expectations about the future—that community asks for and gets chaos."[15]

> Fatherlessness may soon become the defining characteristic of American childhood.

Now, over fifty years after his predictions, Moynihan's warning proved to be frighteningly accurate. Since 1965, the number of fatherless children and the percentage of single families have more than doubled. We now live with the fatherless generation he predicted, and the chaos Moynihan foresaw is rapidly unfolding before us.

Today the destruction is widespread. For the last five decades, the percentage of fatherless children in America has exponentially increased. If the current trend continues, the number of fatherless children in America will soon eclipse the 50 percent mark. Fatherlessness may soon become the defining characteristic of American childhood.

All of this has a price. Not only is there an emotional and physical toll; there is also a financial cost. The individual lives of the fatherless generation are at stake, as well as all who are around them. As the destructive epidemic of fatherlessness continues to grow, our communities, cities, and nation are drastically affected. In the last decade alone, conservative estimates have American taxpayers spending $112 billion annually on fatherlessness and single-parent homes (over $1 trillion dollars for the decade). These costs are in the areas of antipoverty, criminal justice, and educational programs, to name a few. Dr. Ben Scafidi, principal investigator for these findings, remarks, "This new report shows that public concern about the decline of marriage need not be based only on 'moral' concerns, but that reducing high taxpayer costs of family fragmentation is a legitimate concern of government, policymakers and legislators, as well as community reformers and faith communities."[16]

While many of the fatherless act out in desperation, others silently erode away in sadness. When this enduring sadness becomes habitual, it evolves into depression, which *The American Heritage Dictionary* describes as "a mental condition of gloom or sadness, dejection." Specifically, children from fatherless homes are nearly four times more likely to experience major depression in adulthood, over two and a half times more likely to experience bipolar disorders, and nearly four times more likely to experience schizophrenia.[17]

The longer the father wound is ignored or buried, the more it tends to fester. For some, tragically, this depression paves the black road to suicide, which is the ultimate form of despair. One blogger, Wake Up, shared his story with me:

> Nearly three years of life have been filled with anger, hate, and desperation.... February 2008, my father was sentenced to forty years in prison without parole.
>
> From that point on, I tried whatever I could to rid myself of thoughts that I had of my father. As many victims of abuse do,

I turned to drugs, sex, whatever.... It started with partying and the occasional joint, and within six months it turned to ... meth, xanan, cocaine ... and everything between. Addiction, depression, addiction, depression. June 2008, I attempted suicide. As many pills as my mouth could hold. I told no one. The next month, I attempted to quit drugs altogether. So I unknowingly searched for any other kind of high I could put myself under. Shoplifting is where I found it.... Until in July, I was caught with nine CDs from a Target. With cash in the wallet to pay for them. I was processed through the Sunrise, Florida juvenile system.... Until I dropped out of high school in November. I lost nearly all of my closest friends and kept all the dealers I could.... [In rehab] I slowly learned how to deal. How to deal with the pain, the cravings, and the hate....

I use music and writing to get through. Right now I'm working on my debut album. Some sort of an exorcism. Telling my story. Trying to let people into who I am.*

I remember the oil-covered images from the *Exxon Valdez* spill, as the ship ran aground and dumped over 10 million gallons of crude oil into the Prince William Sound off the coast of Alaska in 1989. Experts labeled the spill as the worst human-caused disaster to ever occur at sea. I remember seeing sea otters, harbor seals, sea birds, bald eagles, and killer whales choking on the black poison and dying. Hundreds of thousands of them died. The marine population and local ecosystem collapsed. Businesses were affected; people lost their jobs. Today, over twenty years later, the region is still feeling its effects.

I remember feeling helpless as I watched the birds coated in the black oil, fighting for their lives. Thousands of birds were just sitting there, heaped in large groups, unable to fly. They were trying

---

* Visit *www.myspace.com/thefatherlessgeneration*, "Tell Your Story."

to stretch out their wings, which were too greasy and heavy to allow them to do so. When they tried to preen and clean themselves, they ingested oil, which led to dehydration. The birds couldn't do anything but sit and wait to die.

The fallout from fatherlessness is more than an individual tragedy. It impacts more than the fractured family, the single mother and her children. Fatherlessness is a catastrophic wreck that is poisoning our families, communities, and nation. No one remains unaffected.

AN UNFOLDING PROPHECY

Long before Senator Moynihan's dire predictions of the consequences of a fatherless society, the prophet Malachi predicted the curse that will be unleashed if fathers reject their children. According to the prophecy, which emerges in the final verses of the Old Testament, this curse will be an affliction to the nation where fatherlessness and broken relationships abound. The prophet writes, "I will send you the prophet Elijah before that great and dreadful day of the LORD comes. He will turn the hearts of the fathers to their children, and the hearts of the children to their fathers; or else I will come and strike the land with a curse" (Malachi 4:5–6).

Can it be that we are experiencing the harsh reality of that prophecy? Can it be that we are witnessing the kind of fallout Malachi warned against some twenty-five hundred years ago? The hearts of the fathers are not turned to their children; consequently, the hearts of the children are not turned to their fathers. Can it be that we are bearing the full weight of this fatherless curse?

As we take a closer look at this prophecy, we find that in Luke 1:17, Jesus identifies Malachi's "Elijah" as John the Baptist. John's mission was to "make straight" and prepare the way for Jesus (Luke

3:4) by calling people to turn to God and by turning the hearts of the fathers to their children. So in this sense, Malachi's prophecy was specifically fulfilled in time and history in the person of John.

At the same time, Malachi's prophecy is given with the backdrop of "that great and dreadful day of the LORD," which gives it apocalyptic, end-time significance. Although the prophecy was fulfilled in the first century with John, it still holds a present sense and ongoing relevance. There is a current, divine expectation for its fulfillment, which is the reconciliation between fathers and their children. According to the prophecy, this generational reconciliation prepares the way—as John the Baptist did—for the coming day of the Lord. Commenting on Malachi's prophecy, author Gordon Dalbey writes:

> Healing between fathers and children is not simply a psychological exercise to bring greater peace of mind; in fact, it's the essential prerequisite to fulfilling God's purposes on earth. When fathers are reconciled with sons and daughters, God's saving power is released among us; conversely, when fathers and children remain at odds with one another, powers of destruction are beckoned.[18]

We are witnessing the midnight of this generation. This is both a personal tragedy and a widespread epidemic—a fatherless generation determined to devour itself. We are watching the unfolding of prophetic destruction. As we will see, this epidemic plays out in the rage and violence of our fatherless sons and in the decay and promiscuity of our fatherless daughters. The heart of this generation has been torn out and left bleeding on the ground. Seeds of shame and despair have been sown into the gaping wound. And we are reaping the bitter harvest.

CHAPTER 4

THE FATHERLESS GANG

Bruce: "You didn't know my father."

Ducard: "But I know the rage that drives you—that impossible anger strangling your grief until the memory of your loved one is just poison in your veins. And one day you catch yourself wishing the person you loved had never existed so you'd be spared your pain."

from the movie Batman Begins—a conversation between Bruce Wayne and his mentor, Henri Ducard/Ra's al Ghul

IN OCTOBER 2002, Beltway snipers John Muhammad and Lee Boyd Malvo went on a murder rampage that killed ten people and left others injured. For three weeks, the pair drove around the greater Washington, D.C., area, randomly gunning down innocent victims. Schools closed. People locked themselves inside their homes. The entire region was gripped with fear as the nation watched in horror.

Both men were caught and convicted of their crimes. The forty-two-year-old Muhammad was given the death penalty and was executed on November 10, 2009. Muhammad remained defiant until his last breath. The eighteen-year-old Malvo was spared the death penalty and was given a life sentence in prison. In Malvo's trial, it came to light that he was fatherless and loved Muhammad like a father. During the summer of 2002, Malvo wrote a letter to Muhammad's cousin, saying, "Why am I here? There seems for me no purpose. I'm perceived as a walking time bomb waiting to explode. I've had a hard life, believe it or not, no father, and a mother who hates me. All I ask is to be loved for me."[19]

John Malvo was drowning in rejection. In no way does this excuse his actions. Malvo lived by murder and death. But his personal story is a tragic one. As a fatherless boy, Malvo was crying out for acceptance and for a father. His father hunger was not filled by a father or a loving mentor but by an opportunistic, ruthless killer, John Muhammad. Muhammad became Malvo's deadly "mentor," often introducing Malvo to others as his "son." Muhammad's ultimate plan was to drive across Canada and visit foster homes and YMCAs to recruit, mentor, and train for violence dozens of other fatherless boys just like Malvo.[20]

Like Malvo, a fatherless boy looks to anyone who will accept him and be proud of him. The boy continually seeks validation as a man. If he is fortunate, the person he finds may be a caring mentor, grandfather, or coach — or, sadly, a gang member, drug dealer, or worse.

Left unguided, the boy will usually find a way to vent his frustration and anger. A peer or gang member may even guide him into violent ways of expressing his anger. "In the case of fathers," David Blankenhorn writes, "absence does not make the heart grow fonder. Our intense resentment of fathers is less a result of his presence than of his absence. We abhor him in part because we do not know him."[21]

FATHERLESS RAGE

A fatherless child often rebels against authority, for it represents the sacred position his father once held. Authority is something to be avoided, mocked, or scorned. My friend Pamela—who is deeply invested in mentoring in Portland—told me a disturbing story of a seven-year-old fatherless boy who carved "I hate you" into the leather car seat of his mother's boyfriend's Explorer. From his story, I gathered that this child may well have harbored a hidden hostility toward masculine authority—the result of an absent father. Violent behavior was an outlet for his anger and hostility toward authority.

Distrustful of authority, fatherless boys leave behind a wake of failed jobs and failed relationships. Each of these may start well, but they are inevitably sabotaged by his distrust and rebellion. With the passing of each, he blames his boss, pastor, manager, girlfriend, or spouse. But without knowing it, he is the common denominator in the long line of failed relationships.

Jeremy Shockey, a four-time Pro Bowl tight end with the Giants and the Saints, is well known for talent on the football field and for his angry tirades off of it. Shockey is listed at six foot five, 250 pounds, and has long, wild blond hair and arms that are sleeved with tattoos. At Super Bowl XLIV in Miami, he caught the go-ahead touchdown pass as the New Orleans Saints defeated the Indianapolis Colts for their first ever Super Bowl win. But on the first day of NFL training camp as a rookie, Shockey got into a fistfight with his teammate Brandon Short that ended up breaking bottles, tables, and everything else that got in their way.

Shockey has routinely lambasted television commentators, as well as his own coaches, past and present. During his tenure in the

NFL, it has been common to see him involved in a skirmish or being the instigator of a fight.

As Jeremy revealed to writer S. L. Price in an in-depth *Sports Illustrated* article titled "The Revenge of Jeremy Shockey," Jeremy's father left when he was three. Somewhere along the way, his sadness over his father's absence was replaced by burning rage. Jeremy and his brother grew up dreaming about who would be first to punch Dad in the face. In the interview, Jeremy talked about his fiery motivation:

> Everybody who's ever done anything bad to me, anything that ever went wrong, I try to take it out on somebody—every game.... I couldn't picture myself doing anything else. I'm not out there just doing my job. I take everything personally. A guy beat me up five years ago? If I find [him], I'll get him back.[22]

Talking about his father still gets Jeremy ticked off. He doesn't want his dad to get any credit for his success. To Jeremy, he is a "no one" who deserves nothing. So Jeremy pours his fatherless rage into football. In the article, Price concludes:

> Shockey is the perfect name for what Jeremy is and does. It's also something that maybe, just maybe, will bring his father pain.... Each time Jeremy runs someone down, each time he makes news or hits the gossip columns, he may as well be balling up a fist and cocking his arm. It's not the sweet punch he and his brother have waited so long to throw, but it's revenge all the same.

GANG VIOLENCE AND CIVIL WAR

During the summer of 2008, I had a conversation with evangelist Luis Palau about fatherless youth and rage as we drove from Portland to Rooster Rock National Park, where he was speaking at a youth gathering. I shared with him some of the responses I was getting at my blog, and we began talking about youth and gangs. After Luis shared his own fatherless story, he described a group of young men in New Mexico and Texas who call themselves "the fatherless gang."

Luis told me about his conversation with one of the gangsters, a thirteen-year-old boy who called in to his radio show. He said that the boy joined the gang for protection and to find a family. When Luis asked him how many fatherless boys were in his gang, the boy responded, "About four hundred." Four hundred fatherless boys in Los Cruces, New Mexico, and El Paso, Texas, huddled together in the name of belonging to something, lashing out violently against authority and against their communities.

Sadly, thousands of boys are joining gangs across the country. Many of them are fatherless boys who are lost, seeking protection from enemies and identity from peers. These boys are looking for families — and for fathers. All too often, these young gang members find themselves behind bars, throwing their future away before it ever begins.

There are many contributing factors to the formation of gangs. Socioeconomic hardship, a response to decades of racism, and the growing drug industry have all played a part in creating this complex problem. However, when we take a closer look at the individual stories of gang members, a resounding theme emerges in each. In Stacy Peralta's penetrating documentary *Crips and Bloods: Made in America*, former gang member Kumasi states, "The common thread throughout all of these conversations, throughout our communities, seems to be, for the most part, the absence of a father, a male figure, a father figure in the home."[23]

No matter how loving and competent his mother is, a boy is attracted to a gang by his desire to pull away and enter the world of men. He wants to belong. At the same time, this boy may be sick of being rejected. He may burn with fatherless rage. He may distrust authority. His heart is a mixed bag of rage and rejection, desiring both belonging and rebellion.

The choices he is asked to make are muddled. Does he stay at home, filled with rage and restlessness? Or does he join the gang—entering a community of young men who will show him how to use his strength, albeit in a violent and destructive way? Gang member Shaka of the Mad Swan Bloods said, "I joined the gang not only for the protection but for the love, for the unity, to be a part of a family."[24]

In 2004, I was honored to serve Billy Graham as his multi-language coordinator. During that time, I attended a breakfast where the Los Angeles assistant police chief, Earl Paysinger, was making a plea to some two hundred Hispanic pastors to intervene in the swelling gang problem in South Central Los Angeles. According to Paysinger, a survey by the Los Angeles Police Department revealed some 90,000 registered gang members in Los Angeles County. In the five years from 2000 to 2004, there were nearly 6,000 homicides in Los Angeles County alone. As of December 2009, this figure represents nearly 2,000 more deaths than the total number of U.S. casualties in the Iraq War. Unlike the tragic deaths of our valiant soldiers, these deaths were senseless — and many of them were gang-related.

Paysinger asked the obvious question: "So who are these young men who call themselves 'gangs,' who rape, pillage, and devour our communities?" He responded: "They are young men existing on the fringes of society from broken homes. Their fathers are gone. Many are institutionalized in prison, stuck in the muck and mire, unable to provide training, guidance, and nurturing assistance that gives their sons a chance at a healthy life."[25]

The rampant spread of gangs in our country is the direct result of fatherlessness. Demographically speaking, the most reliable predictor for gang activity and youth violence is neither social class nor race or education — but fatherlessness. No longer do we have to travel abroad to find war; America is making war on itself.

As a nation, we can continue to build more and bigger prisons. But while we spend millions of dollars to imprison these young men, we continue to see the inevitable cycle of fatherless rage churning before our eyes. Our country is at a crossroads. If we continue to focus on the symptom — the rise of gangs and youth violence — we will miss the real problem, the reason why these gangs exist in the first place: *absent fathers.*

CHAPTER 5

FORGOTTEN FAIRY TALES

Fields of wilted flowers
On broken stems,
Hanging, dangling, waiting
For the sun to come, for anyone;
But he is gone, gone far beyond return.

John Sowers

Because of you
I find it hard to trust not only me, but everyone around me
Because of you
I am afraid.[26]

from the song "Because of You," by Kelly Clarkson

IN JUNE 2008, *Time* magazine broke a story titled "Pregnancy Boom at Gloucester High," in which at least seventeen high school girls in Gloucester, Massachusetts, allegedly formed "a pregnancy pact," agreeing to become mothers before finishing high school. Through-out the course of the school year, these girls repeatedly took pregnancy tests from the school nurses, expecting and hoping for babies. When the news story broke, it created an international media firestorm. The magazine interviewed the school principal for his reaction:

> As summer vacation begins, seventeen girls at Gloucester High School are expecting babies.... Principal Joseph Sullivan knows at least part of the reason there's been such a spike in teen pregnancies in this Massachusetts fishing town.... All it took was a few simple questions before nearly half the expecting students, none older than sixteen, confessed to making a pact to get pregnant and raise their babies together. Then the story got worse. "We found out one of the fathers is a twenty-four-year-old homeless guy," the principal says, shaking his head.[27]

For weeks after the story, media outlets feuded over whether such a pact was actually made and discussed the necessity for schoolwide condom distribution. The mayor fueled the debate by saying that there was no hard-core evidence of a pact. But the resigning principal stuck by his claim that there was some kind of agreement held to by at least half of the girls. But the true story got derailed. Lost in the chaos and debate was the fact that seventeen high school girls—none older than sixteen—at Gloucester High School were pregnant.

In a story published on *National Review Online* titled "An Illegitimate Culture," columnist Kathleen Parker brings us back to the important question:

> Where's Dad? Not the "fathers" of these unfortunate pre-borns, but the fathers of these pregnant girls. Where, in other words, is the shotgun?
>
> Back in the day when birth control and abortion weren't readily available to high school kids, fathers were pretty good deterrents to pregnancy. Boys knew they'd have kneecap problems if they got daddy's little girl pregnant....

Today, using the term "illegitimate" is more likely to spark disapproval than the activities contributing to the plague of unwed pregnancies. For sure there are far fewer fathers around to give young males The Eye. It is a fair guess, though not possible to confirm ... that at least some of Gloucester's pregnant daughters are from fatherless homes.

That guess is founded on sound social science indicating a strong correlation between father absence and a high risk for early sex and unwed pregnancy. Not only do fathers provide the masculine affection so many girls seek elsewhere, but they teach their daughters how to handle male sexual aggression, as well as to understand their own role in stimulating that aggression.[28]

Perhaps the real scandal of this story is the fact that it is not an uncommon one. Around 750,000 teenage girls will become pregnant this year. Seventy-one percent of these pregnancies will be from fatherless homes, and over three-fourths unplanned. Nearly a third of these pregnancies will end in abortion, leaving us with some 250,000 teenage abortions each year.[29]

For the teenage mothers who heroically choose to have their babies, most will never return to full-time education. Approximately two out of three babies born to unmarried teens, who have dropped out of high school, are now living in poverty. In contrast, only 7 percent of children born to married high school graduates aged twenty or older are living in poverty.[30] Most of these teenage mothers will end up alone, with the fathers wanting nothing to do with their children.

But how does a girl ever get to this place?

THE DEATH OF A DREAM

In the beginning, every girl longs to be Daddy's little girl. Daddy is the first man to whom she gives and from whom she receives love. Daddy is the man who shapes the way she sees herself. Daddy is the man who develops her worth and identity. She dreams of having his unspoiled attention. Dreams of being the shining princess of his fairy-tale land. Dreams of forever being his precious little girl.

Fatherlessness wilts the dream of being Daddy's little girl.

Through a series of bizarre events that could only happen in Los Angeles, my wife and I became

> Fatherlessness wilts the dream of being Daddy's little girl.

friends with pop star Kelly Clarkson.* As we've spent time with Kelly, we've been impressed with her profound and selfless generosity. She relentlessly gives her time, her heart, and her enthusiasm to friends and family and often engages in projects that help make a difference in the world. We count ourselves blessed to see her heart and to occasionally catch glimpses of her story.

One such glimpse was given to the world in her bestselling song "Because of You." To date, the song has sold over eight million copies in all formats and was one of the hits on Kelly's Grammy-winning album *Breakaway*. The song was so popular that she was asked to perform it at the 2006 Grammy Awards and later recorded a duet version of the song with country music legend Reba McEntire.

My wife, Kari, and I had sushi with Kelly and her band during the Los Angeles leg of her recent tour. We asked Kelly why she thought that there was such a powerful connection to "Because of You." Kelly answered:

> It's a song that hits really close to home for me. A lot of people can relate to this song, even if it's hard. I think it's important for people to see that kind of raw emotion, that kind of heartbreak, because

---

* We met Kelly through her brother, Jason, who has this really great but subdued faux hawk. We exchange texts about the Dallas Cowboys and the Boston Red Sox. Strength and honor Jason.

it happens in real life. Even though I have grown through the pain of my experience, I can still relate to the pain of the song. Tons of people have told me that this song brings out those same emotions in them and that they can see themselves in the video. I think people relate to this song because it puts words to their experience and maybe, in a way, speaks for them.[31]

In the music video, there is a scene in which a young Kelly is playing tug-of-war with her father, clinging to him as he is leaving. She latches on to his suitcase in a final desperate attempt to make him stay. The father stops, jerks her hand off the suitcase, then gets into his car and drives away forever.

As Kelly portrays in the video, the departure of Dad for many young girls can be violent and disruptive. Without Dad's affirmation, daughters grow up struggling with their sense of worth. They feel deficient, that something is lacking. A fatherless daughter may blame herself for what has happened and wonder, "If my father doesn't love me, am I really lovable at all?" One fatherless blogger, Freck!es Normit, comments, "My father has never been part of my life.… Father's Day comes and goes by, and it doesn't faze me. I only know what it means from what I witness with my friends. I am not bitter, but it is sad that I lost the chance to have a male role model who would watch over me and I could be Daddy's little girl."*

> The fatherless daughter's heart goes into hiding beneath the floorboards below. It beats incessantly with the fear of rejection and abandonment.

As in Edgar Allen Poe's "The Tell-Tale Heart," the fatherless daughter's heart goes into hiding beneath the floorboards below. It

---

* Visit *www.myspace.com/thefatherlessgeneration*, "Tell Your Story."

beats incessantly with the fear of rejection and abandonment. After being burned deeply by her father, she loses trust in anyone and everyone. She may be paralyzed by distrust, unable to receive love from a man.

Another blogger, Kathryn, shares this story:

> I did grow up with a daddy, but one day he just snapped. He told my mum he wanted a divorce to go with a younger woman (a family friend.) It also was on my mum's birthday.
>
> I loved my daddy very much when I was little. He hugged me all the time and whispered in my ears that he loved me and that he'll never let me fall from his arms. That changed.... I was alone, scared, confused, young, terrified. I hated everyone at that time. I lost trust in everyone.... I hated both of my parents for years and years. But now, I am stronger. I haven't forgiven them yet, but I'm trying.... I haven't heard from my dad in over four years. I used to sit next to the phone for a call; now I've lost all hope. I don't hate him, but I can't forgive him. I was his little girl. He was the best daddy in the world. Now he is nothing; he is out of my life.*

Scores of girls are still waiting anxiously for Dad to call, even though he has been gone for years. They wait, hoping one day he will acknowledge their existence.

FATHERLESS DAUGHTERS AND PROMISCUITY

The underlying desire for affirmation and approval means many fatherless daughters have trouble making decisions, unable to distinguish between the strong feelings they have and common sense. Young girls may become emotionally promiscuous with any man who pays attention to them. Wandering blindly, they are driven by a need for Dad. They unfold their hearts to other men, hoping to be found and rescued. Their pain leads them into destructive relationships where feelings of shame will surface. These feelings are welcomed, and maybe in a twisted sense are all that she knows.

The fatherless daughter is on a quest to belong. Her wilting heart guides her choices, wishing to be found again. Unguided and unprotected, she lets herself be used, even abused. She gives herself away in promiscuous relationships, looking for Dad. Monique Robinson, author and pastor at Faithful Central Bible Church in Los Angeles, says this about the fallout from her own fatherlessness:

> When my father walked out of my life, confusion stepped in. I never believed in myself. I was fearful of life and fearful of death. In relationships, I longed for love and would do anything to prevent a man from leaving me. I lost my virginity to keep my first boyfriend from breaking up with me and subsequently equated sex with love. Men thought I was cool because whatever they wanted — time, sex, money, a meal — I provided. I viewed the inevitable end of these relationships as abandonment.[32]

The correlation between promiscuous fatherless daughters and teenage pregnancies is obvious. These fatherless girls are the majority of those who are having out-of-wedlock, unintended babies. They are also the ones walking the school hallways or lingering in the office break rooms, sending out signals, looking for adoration and approval. One fatherless blogger, Ramona, writes about her experience:

> I'm nineteen years old, and the first time I met my father was when I was twelve. I have his phone number at this time and give him calls off and on. I recently moved to California from Oregon to be closer to family, when I found out I'm three months pregnant. The father of my child is twenty-six and lives with his mother in Oregon and is fatherless himself. Instead of looking at his father and saying he doesn't want to be like that, he tells me tons of lies

and gives me false hope. I understand that he is not ready for a child but sometime you have to grow up and mature a little. So I live with my mother and am closer to friends, but unfortunately my baby will be fatherless.*

In Northeast Portland, one of my good friends, Duke, started an unconventional church called "Bread and Wine." The church consists of several different groups of people he calls "Gospel Communities." Basically, these groups, called *tribes*, eat together, pray and study the Bible together, serve together, and play together. Sometimes they go to the Laundromat and help wash everyone's clothes. Other times Duke gets them in a big group, and they ride around on their bikes, feeding the homeless and the shut-ins.

> While our fatherless sons rage, our fatherless daughters decay.

On the last Thursday of each month, the Alberta Art Walk takes place. But it's different from a traditional Art Walk, in which local artists hang up their latest paintings while everyone mills around with a glass of Pinot in their hand. Instead, it's a smorgasbord of characters: folk singers, gypsies, homeless youth, fire dancers, and carnies.

Duke and his crew set up a table in the middle of all the madness, hang a poster board on their table that reads, "Tell Your Story," and for several hours sit and listen to people. People typically line up at the table by the dozens to share. Sometimes the stories are tragic; sometimes they are hopeful.

A couple months back, Duke was moved by a story he heard from three girls, ages fourteen to sixteen. Each had convinced an older

* Visit *www.myspace.com/thefatherlessgeneration*, "Tell Your Story."

guy (in his midtwenties) that she was eighteen so that she could sleep with him. Duke said that the girls acted amused as they shared this. But they were also visibly insecure and nervous, speaking through forced laughter as if they were daring Duke to reject them.

At one point, the conversation slowed down and the girls got really honest. They saw how unhealthy it was and how lonely and empty their lives had become. After a pause, the youngest spoke for the group: "It's amazing how not having a father has affected all of us." Then she asked Duke and his wife, Caroline, for help. Caroline was able to share her story with the girls, saying later that she felt something helpful was imparted to them. Duke told me they were begging for parents, asking him to give them the acceptance and direction they hadn't received from their missing fathers.

While our fatherless sons rage, our fatherless daughters decay.

Driven by a crippling sense of unworthiness and a gnawing hunger for Dad, they are emotionally and sexually promiscuous. Every year, thousands will become pregnant, with many of their babies being aborted. For those who choose to keep their children, the majority of them will be, like their mothers, fatherless.

CHAPTER 6

RUNNING TO STAND STILL

[The demon-possessed man] lived there among the tombs and graves. No one could restrain him—he couldn't be chained, couldn't be tied down. He had been tied up many times with chains and ropes, but he broke the chains, snapped the ropes. No one was strong enough to tame him. Night and day he roamed through the graves and the hills, screaming out and slashing himself with sharp stones.

Mark 5:3–5 MSG

A FEW MONTHS AGO, I had a conversation with Cameron, a good friend of mine. Cameron is one of those golden guys who can do anything he wants. In high school, he was a two-time national speech finalist. He can act, and he can write.

Cameron is also a recovering drug user.

I recently asked Cameron to tell me his story—how he happened to start down the road to drug abuse. Our conversation went like this:

Me: You grew up without a father around. Can you explain a bit about that? What emotions stuck with you from that time?

Cameron: I read somewhere that each of us receives a message from our fathers. My message was: *You will never be as important to me as the women in my life.* I always felt second-rate. I never took priority. I was just there as a garnish, moved off the plate and onto the napkin, quickly disposed of, nice to look at but never edible. It was like I was his civic obligation. "Well, I have to see my son again, so I might as well make the most of it. Might as well go ahead and do jury duty while I'm at it."

Me: How did this affect the way you related to other people?

Cameron: When it came to friends, which crowd did I belong to? I frantically moved from crowd to crowd because I felt too embarrassed, too ashamed, to stand up and be anyone of definitive substance. When it came to dating and women, I was absolutely crippled. I could never overcome my insecurities, doubts, and fears, which led me to push women away before they could reject me.

Me: How did this experience shape the way you saw yourself?

Cameron: Whenever I was around my dad, he constantly showed me what I was *not*. My father was an athlete; I was not. My father was a ladies' man; I was not. My father was brilliant; I never felt intelligent—not ever—and especially never around him. After a lifetime of feeling stupid in front of him, I brought home my future bride, and all he said about her was: "She's very intelligent." The only thing I was good at was acting. But I always felt like he saw that as gay. No matter what I did, I could never make him proud. Everything I've ever done, I think somewhere, deep down, I did to make him proud. But I couldn't.

Me: How did your drug use come about?

Cameron: I began using drugs and alcohol when I was fifteen years old. My first time was with my cousin on my father's side. Everything I ever did that was wrong, I think I did with him first. I don't really know why. We were both fatherless, and we were related, so that meant something to us. For some reason, I admired my cousin beyond words. When he was around, I would sit and soak up all that I could. I was *learning* him. When he left, I *became* him.

But I felt horribly guilty. I used drugs, and then I'd go down to the altar at church to repent and rededicate. After I went to college, I began using alcohol and drugs as a coping mechanism, a way of escape, if only for a moment. But the pain wouldn't go away. It grew. So I had to have more drugs to cope with it. Funny how that worked — the more I used drugs to escape, the more I needed to escape and the more I needed to escape from. I surrounded myself with drugs, pills, drinks, music, women, friends, clothes, image. All these things made a noise, a clamor. Anything to block out the pain, anything to block out God's voice. I filled my heart with anger and bitterness so no one could get in. I met a lot of different people at that time, but no one ever knew who I was. I didn't even know myself. I lived the lie until the lie became the truth.

Me: What finally woke you up?

Cameron: At the height of the drugs and drinking and women, I got arrested and thrown in jail for drug abuse. But sadly, being arrested wasn't the rock-bottom point for me. In some ways it was just the beginning. After getting arrested, I moved to Springfield from Florida and lived with my father for a summer. During this time I tried to connect with him on a different level. I wanted him to reach out to me, but I acted like I didn't care.

I think I was sober all of one week that summer. I smoked weed and/or drank every day. I worked as a sauté cook at an Italian restaurant and showed up to work stoned and worthless. One night I was at a house party and stayed up smoking weed and came home the next morning as my dad was leaving for work. Neither of us said anything to each other. I wanted him to say something.

That entire summer was an escape for me. I tried to quench the burning fear and my self-loathing with another fix. I tried to drown the desperation and anxiety I had about my upcoming court trial—I truly didn't know whether or not I'd end up in prison doing hard time. Because of the drug charges, I had two felonies hanging over my head—easily qualifying me for prison time.

That summer with my dad, I became another person. I was never the same when I returned to Florida in the fall. When the court finally decided my fate, I avoided prison and was placed on probation. But instead of turning around or waking up, I went deeper into drugs than ever before. What was once a cocaine addiction turned into meth.

I hit rock bottom a lot. And I would cry out to God. I would promise, "This is the last time. I'm turning around. I'm going to get right." But it never took. That was the hardest part for me. I felt like, *It has never worked before. Why is it going to work now?*

I finally just gave up. I assumed the inevitability of my failure. But amazingly, I knew that God was still there for me. I also knew that I needed to be around some Christian people to help me, so I joined the Christmas play at church. Keeping busy with the play and working full-time, I grew apart from my old party buddies. Waking up from my drug coma wasn't anything magical. God just wore me down. Actually, he just knew the right time and situation for me to be willing to listen. And to do that, he had to lead me to people who would accept me—failures, past, habits, everything—and see the real me behind it all. And love me anyway.

The themes of Cameron's story seem like a rhythmic progression: rejection, conformity, destruction. As an actor, Cameron soon found himself living a life of deception and drug abuse. His entire life became one big act: "I lived the lie until the lie became the truth." But in a dramatic sense of irony, God interrupted that pattern. God used Cameron's love of acting to bring him back from the brink. Not many people sign up for the Christmas play with the idea of turning away from a life of drugs. Cameron's story and his involvement with drugs led me to explore the connections between fatherlessness, drug use, and self-destructive behaviors.

FATHERLESSNESS AND DRUG ABUSE

Why is it that 75 percent of all drug users come from fatherless homes? Why are nearly 65 percent of all suicides from fatherless homes? What is it about fatherlessness that causes young people to hate and destroy themselves? In some respects, the fatherless experience echoes the biblical story of the demon-possessed man, known only as Legion (Mark 5). The name refers to a typical Roman squadron of soldiers, usually numbering approximately six thousand men. This man, tormented by thousands of demons, would spend his days howling in anguish as he slashed himself with rocks.

Though the Scriptures don't give us much detail about his life, I cannot help but wonder about the backstory of this man who lived with the oppression of such evil. At some point, it would seem that he became a problem for the community, a nuisance. Scorned by his hometown, his neighbors, and everything he knew as familiar, he was labeled, rejected, bound and chained near the cliffs and left for dead. All alone, he gave himself over to the gnawing darkness. He lost his name. He lost his sanity. Defined by the identity of his tormentor, Legion was doomed to live in the catacombs until he, too, became one of the forgotten dead.

> What is it about fatherlessness that causes young people to hate and destroy themselves?

Like Legion, many of the fatherless embrace physical pain to erase the inner, emotional pain. Illogically, they hurt themselves so that the pain will stop. Some use the pain to escape, to avoid reality. But pain is a terrible companion. He's greedy. He's never satisfied, never sated or fulfilled. For the fatherless, pain is a dirty needle in a broken vein, a cold razor pressed into the flesh, lines of white powder on a mirror.

Whatever manifestation pain takes, those who live with the pain of fatherlessness often limp through their days in silent agony. The U.S. Department of Health and Human Services was already warning us back in 1993 that children from fatherless homes have a dramatically greater risk of drug and alcohol abuse.[33] Now we are seeing the fruit of fatherlessness everywhere we look.

> Pain is a terrible companion. He's greedy.

Tiffany, a fatherless girl I met on my blog, writes:

> I self-medicated with lots and lots and lots of drugs and alcohol. I was addicted to heroin by the time I was seventeen years old. No one ever says, "I want to be a junkie when I grow up." I hit rock

bottom in 2001 when I was strung out on heroin, stealing from family, friends, and strangers — putting whatever money I had in my veins or up my nose. I was in an abusive relationship. I was living in a bad movie about sex, drugs, rock 'n' roll, and violence. I attempted to kill myself over and over again. But I proved to myself that I couldn't even do that right.*

One of the things I remember most about kindergarten was show-and-tell. Usually I brought in something fairly typical, like a baseball glove or a frog. I don't remember anyone's dreams or what they wanted to be when they grew up, but I can guess what they might have said. A fireman. A cowboy. A princess. A rock star. I'm fairly certain I never heard a classmate tell the class, "I wanna try drugs and become a junkie. Maybe one day, I'll try to kill myself." None of us intentionally decide we want to destroy our life. You aren't going to find a kindergartener bragging about wanting to use meth when he grows up. I think the journey to self-destruction is a process of slow degeneration, not necessarily an impulsive choice.

FATHERLESSNESS AND SELF-DESTRUCTION

Jason, who was six when his dad left, blogs about his self-destructive story:

> At twenty-six I swallowed my first ecstasy tablet, turned to amphetamines and speed, and developed a cocaine habit. Lonely and depressed, I spiraled further and further down to a state of absolute hopelessness....
>
> That's when I decided I had had enough. I was in the bath ready to commit suicide with a knife. I had left a note on the door to say "don't enter," shutting it tight. Somehow Moonie, my white Staffy bull terrier, opened the door and came bolting in! Knocking

---

* Visit *www.myspace.com/thefatherlessgeneration*, "Tell Your Story."

the knife off the bath, my dog brought me to my senses. I just couldn't do it — my dog saved my life.*

Several experts believe there is a strong connection between fatherlessness and self-injury or "cutting." A fatherless generation blogger, Natasha, said she cuts herself when she gets depressed. Her father moved away when she was six. She still writes her dad countless letters, but he never writes back. She says, "I must be horrible … if my father never wants to see me. Isn't it normal for a father to want to see his own daughter? What could I have done to make him hate me so much?" Whenever the pain is too much, she reaches for her razor.

I met Jamie Tworkowski a few months back over breakfast in Los Angeles. Jamie leads a growing movement called "To Write Love on Her Arms" (TWLOHA). A lot of young people struggle with cutting, depression, drug addiction, and suicidal thoughts, and in the last couple of years, Jamie and his team have connected with millions of young people through a simple message of hope. Jamie recently won an MTV Woodie Award for his work with TWLOHA.

When I asked Jamie about the connections between drug abuse, self-injury, and fatherlessness, he said, "We hear from so many young people who feel alone in their pain. They write to us, sharing the hardest parts of their story, asking real questions for the first time. In a perfect world, they would grow up with a father they could look to for love and strength and wisdom, but so many don't have that. And so they grow up having no idea how to have an honest conversation or how to ask for help, because they've never seen it modeled."

Jamie also told me that two out of three people who struggle with depression never get help. He comments, "Untreated depression

---

* Visit *www.myspace.com/thefatherlessgeneration*, "Tell Your Story."

is the leading cause of suicide, so the stakes could not be higher. One of the biggest things we've learned after hearing thousands of these stories is that young people desperately need their fathers. They need family and friendship and community. We treasure every story we hear and are honored to come alongside these young people and connect them to hope and community."

The fatherless generation embraces pain to escape the anguish of a missing father. They believe and live the lies of rejection until the lie becomes the truth. Like Legion, they isolate themselves to escape the pain through drugs or self-injury—sometimes even suicide. They have forgotten their own names and have become hell-bent on destroying themselves.

And they are crying out for help.

PART TWO

REDEEMIN THE STORY

CHAPTER 7

RETURNING THE FAVOR

I have difficulty praying the Lord's Prayer because whenever I say "Our Father," I think of my own father, who was hard, unyielding, and relentless. I cannot help but think of God that way.

Martin Luther

IT HAS BEEN SAID that God created man in his image, and man returned the favor. Our natural impulse is to view God through the lens of the relationship we had with our earthly father. For those of us who had attentive and faithful fathers, our memories of him may conjure up feelings of warmth, security, and strength. It is not a stretch for us to imagine God in that same way. For others, though, with absent or abusive fathers, the very word *father* can be a razor-wire barrier to knowing God.

For the fatherless, accepting the idea that God is a loving Father is difficult. Don Miller writes, "My father left my home when I was young, so when I was introduced to the concept of God as Father I imagined him as a stiff, oily man who wanted to move into our house and share a bed with my mother. I can only remember this as a frightful and threatening idea."[34]

Recently I had a conversation with a fatherless teenage girl who was seated next to me on a flight from Denver to Springfield, Missouri. She was around fourteen, with a decidedly Goth vibe — jet-black hair and some facial piercings. She told me she thought God was whoever we made him out to be, and the idea of God as Father was repulsive to her. God could be a man or woman, an impersonal "higher power," or anything else we wanted him or her to be.

After listening to her vent for a while, I decided to ask her what she thought about my hair. Not surprisingly, she thought it was kind of boring. But eventually she agreed with me that it was short and brown, with a sort of steel-wool texture. We went on until we had a pretty good physical description of me: six foot two, brown hair and eyes, dashing good looks, and the like.

I then asked her if someone *thought* I was actually seven feet tall instead of six foot two, would I magically grow ten inches or stay exactly the same? Would I actually change every time people thought differently about me, or was this a problem with perception?* Then I asked her if she thought that God changed every time we thought differently of him. I wish I could say she was won over by my argument. She wasn't. But I think my point made her think a little.

In his brilliant book *Faith of the Fatherless*, New York University professor Paul Vitz applies what he terms "the defective father hypothesis" to the lives of over twenty well-known atheists.[35] Vitz takes a close look at Freud's projection theory, which declares that belief in God is a psychological result of being raised in a home with a good father. Vitz argues that if we are going to accept Freud's

---

* *Merriam-Webster's Collegiate Dictionary* defines *distortion* as "a lack of proportionality in an image resulting from defects in the optical system."

"projection theory," we must apply it universally. If those who believe in God believe because they have fathers, then those who do not believe in God must not believe because they lacked fathers. Vitz sees this as true of many of the top atheists of the past few centuries.

Frederick Nietzsche's father, a Lutheran pastor, died a couple of months before Nietzsche's fifth birthday. Nietzsche writes in detailed sadness of the day of his father's death. Later in his life, Nietzsche famously proclaimed, "God is dead." Noted atheist David Hume lost his father when he was only two. Atheist Bertrand Russell is well known for his essay titled "Why I Am Not a Christian." Russell's father died when he was four. Philosopher and atheist Jean-Paul Sartre's father died when he was fifteen months old. Albert Camus's father died in World War I when Albert was an infant. Camus later writes in detail about his own search for a father.

I am not saying that Freud's hypothesis is correct. I am living proof that it is not. But both he and Vitz have a relevant point. Our fathers powerfully shape our perception of God—like a projector flinging grainy images on the screen of our minds. Fathers project images of trust and security that inspire faith. Or they project bleak, dark images of rejection, isolation, and abandonment.

FATHERLESSNESS AND THE DEATH OF GOD

If our fathers were absent as we were growing up, we may tend to view God as distant and uncaring. If our fathers were rigid disciplinarians, we may be nervous around God, seeing him as something of a cosmic policeman. If our fathers were flighty and inconsistent, we may write off God as unreliable. If our fathers were abusive, we may fear God's anger. If our fathers left us or died when we were young, we may feel that God, too, is dead in our lives.

Fatherless children often believe that God, like their earthly father, is now gone. He does not inhabit their bleak and ashen existence. He does not speak a meaningful word to their postmodern existence. And this theme—alienation from God—is repeated over and over by young people growing up without their fathers, struggling with their experience of rejection, and trying to understand God in the midst of it all.

A young man in his twenties, Justin, commented:

> I've often wondered what would have been more painful: a father I've never known and never seen or a father I've seen and never known. He never shares what's on his heart.
>
> And the closer I try to get to him, the further away I feel. Why is it that my greatest fear is becoming the man that gave me life? And why do I still seek his approval? Is he the reason it's so hard for me to see God as Father?

Another blogger, a forty-year-old married man and father of two, William, adds:

> I was six when my dad left. My little brother sat on the couch and cried, "I want my daddy," for what seemed like hours and hours. He cried himself to sleep at night. When he was at school, he cried around his classmates. He was so broken that he couldn't really control his emotions at all. But not me. I had to be the strong one. And I swore that day that my dad would never see me cry, nor would anyone else. Not even God. I shut it all in, locked away like a vault. It wasn't until years later that I discovered the problem with that setup. Not only had I locked away the anger and pain; I had locked away everything else too. I completely forgot how to feel.

A third blogger, Michelle, who is a fatherless single mom with three kids, talks about how difficult it was for her to see God as Father. She had been disappointed by every man she had ever known—first by her father, then by her unfaithful husband. She had attended church before, but it had never connected to her heart. For Michelle, seeing God as Father was seemingly impossible:

> I had been to church before, but it never really took. I didn't have a problem with it; I met some great people there. But I had a hard time connecting all the dots. Now, looking back for me, I know that it had everything to do with my fatherless childhood and my husbandless marriage. One day, I was listening to a sermon on the radio, driving the girls home from school, and I was absolutely exhausted by raising the girls, working two dead-end jobs just to make ends meet, exhausted with life in general. I was at my wits end, ready to scream.
>
> As I listened to the sermon, I distinctly remember praying, asking God for one thing: help! I thought he existed, but I had never really tried to pray before. Not anything more than lip service. I wasn't really into men, and God seemed like the King Man. So here I was in the car, asking him for help, when the strangest thing happened. Within seconds, I felt like God was telling me, or showing me, that I was his precious little girl. It's not like I heard him say anything, but I was overwhelmed with his delight for me—I could feel his love. And he had been waiting for me to come to him so that he could pour out tons of affection and grace over me. It's like he had been pursuing me but ultimately waiting for me for years and years to come to him, the perfect gentleman. My eyes filled with tears, and I had to pull the car over. From that day on, God began to make sense. He was no longer an impersonal or scary thought. That day God became my Father, my true love.

One of the great theologians of the twentieth century, A. W. Tozer, once said, "What comes into our minds when we think about God is the most important thing about us."[36] Our perception of God defines who we are and affects the way we relate (or do not relate) to him. We may be confused or angry with God. We may be paranoid about or afraid of him. We may think he is whimsical and inconsistent, or see him as an impersonal, faceless deity.

The way fatherless children see God also affects the way they relate to others, especially men. Having never seen masculine goodness, they may look at it with suspicion. They may begin to fear that divine characteristics such as fidelity, compassion, goodness, and trust simply don't exist. They may begin to believe that all men are villainous.

I saw this restructuring of God play out in my life. I liked my dad but didn't see him much. As I grew older, he grew more and more distant. In my mind, God was much the same way—a swell guy to be sure, but not involved in my life. God was likable but distant, good but aloof.

Growing up this way, I never felt good enough to merit my existence. I convinced myself that I had to *do something* to matter to others. So I became a performer. But it always felt like I was being watched and evaluated by others. With big clipboards and red pens, they were constantly grading my performance.

I projected this performance mind-set onto God. Christianity became something like Little League baseball. God became the coach who cheered for me when I hit well but looked away in silent disapproval when I struck out. I went to Sunday school and did everything I could to be the "good little boy." I found this was my golden ticket to acceptance.

I based my entire worth on my performance. Whenever I screwed up, I was terrified. I kept wondering if and when God's grace would finally run out for me. I constantly wondered, "Am I doing enough? Is this OK? Does God still love me? Have I finally fallen off the edge of grace?" I tiptoed around sheepishly, looking over my shoulder, waiting for God to throw his big, black shoe at the back of my head.

Approaching God like this, based on my performance, made the story more about me than him. I lived in ignorance of God's unconditional acceptance. Before too long, I found myself running in a religious fog, burning out under the weight of it all. I was tired of the constant rules and the pressure and the unrealistic expectations I was placing on myself. It was a religious performance—a tap dance—and God was my audience.

It wasn't until later that God broke through. I realized that relationship with him is not a moral code or a religious performance. It is not a list of rules or a tap dance. It's more like Argentine tango. It's wild, free, and alive. And it invades our personal space.

• • •

In Luke 15, Jesus tells the story of a woman who lost a coin. She must have really valued that coin, because she turned her house upside down looking for it. Most of us don't have coins that are worth destroying our houses over (though I nearly demolished my apartment once, looking for my iPod). Upon closer inspection, we learn that this woman's coin was a drachma, a silver coin worth about a day's wages. So when she loses her coin, her whole life stops. With grim determination and single-minded focus, she begins the search.

She looks everywhere, retracing her steps. She turns over couches, dumps out her piggy bank three times, empties the refrigerator. She crawls around on hands and knees looking for it. When she finally finds it, she lets out a yelp that makes the neighborhood dogs bark. She laughs so hard that she nearly hyperventilates. Then in raw celebration, she calls everyone in her bingo club and tells them about her wonderful discovery.

The fatherless may care nothing about God. They may grow hostile at the mention of his name. They may feel as though religion is a "crutch" and the whole idea of God is foolish. Perhaps they have tried reducing God to a moral code or a performance. Maybe they even believe, like Nietzsche, that God is dead. But regardless of what they may or may not think about God, he is forever thinking of them. And he, like the woman who lost her precious coin, is in stubborn and reckless pursuit of their hearts.

CHAPTER 8

BELONGING TO GOD

*This is and has been the Father's work from the beginning—
to bring us into the home of his heart. This is our destiny.*
George MacDonald, *The Truth in Jesus*

ONE OF MY FAVORITE MUSICIANS is Matt Redman. Matt is an author, singer, and songwriter, and he is one of the most prolific worship leaders in the world. His songs are routinely sung in churches everywhere. Some of the songs he has written are "Heart of Worship," "Better Is One Day," "Facedown," "Blessed Be Your Name," and, my favorite, "You Never Let Go." You don't have to spend a long time hanging around Matt to understand why he is so widely respected. He is soft-spoken and attentive. His humility is disarming, which seems profoundly appropriate for someone who sings about the greatness of God.

I recently asked Matt a few questions about his own experience of growing up without a father—how it impacted his childhood and shaped him as a person. Matt graciously shared his story:

My dad died suddenly when I was seven years old. I found out a few years later that he had actually taken his own life. I guess in some ways it was a double shock, and that brings up a whole lot of new questions: Did it have anything to do with me? Didn't he love us enough to stay around? The older I've become, the more I understand some of the reasons, and the main one is depression, which is a very toxic affliction that pollutes a person's outlook, even the good things. My mum remarried, and things took a turn for the worst—that guy abused our trust as a family, and things stayed very rocky for a few years.

There were definitely a few years of pain and struggle there in my childhood and early teenage years—but to be truthful, I never felt very "fatherless." I think that has a lot to do with God being true to his word. Scripture tells us that he is a Father to the fatherless, and I knew a massive measure of that as I grew up. In fact, so many of the painful things in my childhood, by his grace, propelled me *toward* God and not away from him. I would go so far as to say that these times of turmoil were actually the things that solidified my walk with God and made me want to walk and talk with him. Throughout that whole season, somehow, I had a very real sense of God being my Father—and a very strong and compassionate one at that.[37]

Matt spoke of God being a Father to him, even through the painful loss of his earthly father. As we saw in the previous chapter, the questions and the darkness that the fatherless feel—the "painful things" that haunt them—often drive them *away* from God. But Matt's story takes a different direction. Even during his years of pain and struggle, Matt experienced God's closeness, God "being true to his word."

FATHERLESSNESS AND THE HEART OF GOD

The faithfulness of God is a repeated theme in Scripture, and we learn that there is a special place in the heart of God for the fatherless. The Bible makes it clear that there is one who hears and acts on behalf of those who have been abandoned, a Father who longs to father a rejected generation.

Growing up as a child, my struggle to accept God as Father was not as much conceptual as it was practical. There was never any doubt in my mind that God existed. Nor was there any doubt that he said he was a loving Father. I knew this as much as I was alive. But knowing these things was far different from actually *relating* to God. I had no idea what that looked like. To me, the idea of God as Father was a nice Sunday school idea that had little bearing on the way I actually lived. God was a compartment in my life that I opened and closed for two hours every Sunday morning. I had reduced God to a safe and impersonal idea that I could keep at a distance. I was a Christian in theory but an atheist in practice.

I had prayed the magic prayer when I was eight years old. This prayer, according to my neighbor Tony, would keep me from a fiery and eternal hell. All I had to do was ask Jesus into my heart. It seemed easy enough. To punctuate the urgency of this prayer, Tony warned me that I could never know when I might die. I might choke on a chip at lunch if I didn't pray it immediately. Terrified, I begged God to keep me from going to hell. After we finished praying, Tony patted me on the back and welcomed me into the club. Secure in the knowledge that I was safe from the fire, I went inside and ate my Doritos.

As I grew older, my relationship with God grew into something more than a sterile, onetime cosmic transaction that kept me from burning. Looking back, that simple prayer was more of an introduction to God. It has taken me some time to trust that God will not one day walk out of the door of my life. It has taken time to believe that he will never leave me or forsake me.

I am learning that God loves me and gave the life of his Son for me that I might become his. Jesus willingly chose to experience a divine fatherlessness for me — the pain of rejection on the cross, rejection for my sin — that I might *belong* to the Father.

When I began dealing with the issues of my own fatherlessness, I started writing down my prayers and thoughts in a journal. Over the course of a month, I filled up my blue journal with clippings, articles, sermons, and songs about belonging to God. One of those journal entries read:

> To belong to God means I am no longer defined by what I do, no longer defined by my performance. I am defined by his love for me. Whatever anyone else says about me doesn't really mean jack squat. It is only God that matters.
>
> To belong to God means I am free to approach God with the simplicity of a child. I can share my heart with him the same way I would to my wife or best friend. No prayer is insignificant. I don't have to get whipped up into some emotional lather or bring a fancy prayer to impress him. He's just happy to have me around. I think God receives prayers a lot like the mom who loves the colorings of her preschool toddler. Even though the sun is purple and the grass is red, and none of the colors stayed within the lines, Mom still loves the picture and sticks it proudly on her refrigerator.
>
> To belong to God means I am no longer ashamed. God heals the shame of my fatherlessness through the dignity of adoption. The core experience of my life is no longer rejection. I am accepted. There is no longer something missing inside. I do not have to strive or compete to earn my worth. My shame has been replaced by sonship. I belong to God. Now it's enough to simply *be*.

Some try to transcend the fatherless story, as I did, by becoming a performer. Others sink down into the shame of fatherlessness and wear it as a badge of identity, becoming a victim. But an unfortunate side effect of the victim story line is bitterness. Bitterness is a rot that spreads the longer we hold on to it and nurse our injury.

Belonging to God frees us to let go of our bitterness, our resentment, and our drive to perform. The Bible states, "Forgive as the Lord forgave you" (Colossians 3:13). Forgiveness is a gift from God, a gift that we must pass on to others to truly receive. Forgiving my father and those who have hurt me means I must let go of the victim story. My fatherlessness no longer defines who I am.

GOD IS THERE

I used to have a blue lounge chair that I bought for twenty-five dollars at a garage sale. For years, until I got rid of it, it sat in the corner of the front bedroom of my condo. I wish I still had that chair. It was obnoxiously bright, held together with tarnished brass buttons. The vinyl covering had long cracks that ran like spidery veins. It weighed a ton. It sat next to my beat-up black footlocker, and a couple of guitars kept it company, along with a lonely djembe drum.

Sometimes in the stillness of the early morning or late night, I would slip down to my knees and lay my head softly on that blue chair. It was like God was sitting there in that chair,

> To belong to God means I am no longer ashamed. God heals the shame of my fatherlessness through the dignity of adoption.

my head resting on his lap. I didn't say much in those moments, content just to inhale and exhale, deeply and slowly. After some time, I would sit in the chair, open my Bible, and ask God to speak to me. My soul would be replenished. I prayed about whatever was on my heart. God would quiet my soul, and I would leave those times changed.

When we allow God to enter our lives, the ghost of our father diminishes. There's really no easy way to explain it. But I know that when I get away from the constant noise of my life, my neighbor's loud television, and the frantic hurry of the crowds, God is there.

He's always there. Even if I don't feel him.

And he's not there to demand performance or condemn failures. He's not like the needy friend who calls and always wants to talk for an hour. He is completely selfless. I've had countless one-sided conversations with him. And he just listens to me, quietly and patiently.

I'm still learning how to listen.

CHAPTER 9

FATHER TO THE FATHERLESS

A father to the fatherless, a defender of widows,
   is God in his holy dwelling
God sets the lonely in families....

Psalm 68:5–6

IN THE PREVIOUS CHAPTER, Matt Redman talked about belonging as he shared how God was close to him in his fatherlessness. This was one way in which God fathered him, and it is a significant step of healing for every fatherless child—to experience the divine embrace of their heavenly Father. But Matt also spoke of the men God provided in his life, men who came alongside him, taught him, walked with him, and fathered him. Matt told me, "The other thing that really helped me was seeing God provide many great mentor figures along the way—all throughout my teen years and beyond. In 1 Corinthians 4:15, Paul comments that the Corinthians have had many teachers in Christ—but not many fathers. I'm grateful that this has never been my experience. Though I grew up without a father, I was blessed with an abundance of older guys who invested into my life with words of encouragement and direction, and they set an example for me in the faith."

I can't help but wonder what kind of story Matt would have had if these mentors had not been involved in his life. What if the men who "fathered" Matt Redman had not answered the call? What joys would they have missed? And what kind of person would Matt be today? It's hard to say.

Many of my friends have similar stories of how God has provided mentors in their lives who sacrificially served as coaches, friends, and fathers. These are mentors who had a tremendous impact, mentors who left a quiet legacy, who served without clamor or fanfare, who made a lasting difference.

God fathers us through the intimacy of his Spirit, but also by bringing people—spiritual fathers and mothers—into our lives. These mentors teach us what it is like to be loved, what it means to be a man or woman. A mentor's presence in the life of a young person declares to him or her, "You are not rejected. You are important and valuable—you matter."

God is calling his body, the church, to step up and be *his* people, to represent his fathering love to a fatherless generation of children and youth. And he is giving us opportunities to answer the call. This is the heart of mentoring. Mentoring is about answering God's call, joining with him as he rewrites the broken story of a generation. Mentoring mirrors God's pursuing heart. Long before we ever consider him, God knows us, loves us, and pursues us. As mentors, we follow God by taking the initiative and choosing to invest our time and energy into the life of a child or young person.

• • •

When I was six, my mom signed me up for Big Brothers and Big Sisters in Little Rock. My first "Big" was a friendly guy named Tom. Tom had a crooked smile and black hair slicked over to the side, and to my six-year-old eyes, he was really, really hairy.

The first time we hung out together, Tom took me to the Baskin Robbins ice cream shop. At first, I wasn't sure what to think about this guy, but he dispelled all my worries when he bought me two scoops of chocolate ice cream. From that point on, I was sold. As we drove home in his pickup truck, he whispered that he thought there was a ghost on the roof of the truck. I remember both of us screaming in terror-filled delight.

Several months later, I mustered the courage to ask Tom why he was so hairy. He got this serious look on his face, and I thought I might have offended him. For all I knew, Tom had a freakish disease that made him extra hairy. He pulled over, took a deep breath, looked me right in the eye, and told me his mother was a monkey. Now I wasn't one of those gullible six-year-olds, and I didn't really believe him. Not really. But when a guy opens his heart to you like that, you can't just laugh in his face. Every year afterward, Tom would send me a birthday card with a monkey pictured on the front, and the card would be signed "from Tom and Mom." It was just an inside joke between a boy and his Big Brother—but it was one of those things that made all the difference in the world.

Tom and I continued to hang out a couple of times a month, and about a year later, we went fishing together at Lake Maumelle. We stopped at a place called the Jolly Roger Marina. There was a black skull-and-crossbones flag flying outside the door, and after our visit to the Jolly Roger, our simple fishing trip was transformed into a pirate adventure. For the rest of the weekend, Tom adopted a pirate accent, and we rented a green aluminum boat from ol' Verl behind the counter and set out for the deep seas. By the end of the day, we had only caught a few small fish, but it didn't matter to me. I was loving my new life as a pirate with my Big Brother Tom. As the weekend came to a close, I knew our time was short, so I kept asking Tom for "just one more cast." I'll never forget the last cast of the day, when I landed a largemouth bass weighing several pounds. I went home that day feeling like Blackbeard the pirate lord.

Tom and I continued to hang out a few times a month over the next several years, and eventually he got married. A year or so later, Tom went to seminary to became a Presbyterian preacher, and he now lives in Dallas.

After Tom moved to Texas, I got another Big Brother named Sonny. Sonny was from rural Arkansas and was a rugged hunter. Sonny and I spent a lot of time in the woods, and he taught me how to hunt. The first few times I went deer hunting with Sonny, I didn't carry a rifle or a shotgun. My job was simply to walk along quietly and avoid stepping on leaves or branches. I learned how to stalk and still-hunt. There is something primal that comes alive in a young boy when he is out hunting. All of the senses are heightened. You're able to hear the slightest noise, and your eyes adjust to see in the almost nonexistent early morning light of dawn.

Each night before we went out to hunt, Sonny would look at a topographical map and somehow know where the deer were going to be by the shape of the land, the hills, and the valleys. He could also tell by looking at the map where the bucks would be moving and where the general herd of does and yearlings would be located. Sonny was almost always right. He bought me a rifle, and I killed my first deer when I was eight years old.

The best part of deer hunting, though, was going to deer camp. Deer camp was held at an old, broken-down wooden cabin somewhere in the middle of Nowhere, Arkansas. The bathroom — a graying woodshed about fifty yards from the main cabin — was a dilapidated mess. A campfire burned low, with men hunkered around drinking coffee late into the night, looking into the fire. Usually a deer carcass was hanging up between trees in front of the cabin, like some sort of meaty, headless scarecrow marking the territory of a toothy band of savages. Sometimes coyotes crept up warily to the carcass. I could see their hungry, glowing eyes peering out of the bushes.

There were other wild beasts out and about. Sonny told me of the time he was restocking the corn for a deer feeder when a massive boar suddenly burst out of the brush and charged him. He barely had time to climb a nearby tree. Deer camp was also home to a black mountain lion. While I never saw him, sometimes I could hear him screaming late at night.

Sonny and I kept in touch throughout high school. He came to my football games. Eventually, he got a promotion working for the energy company in another part of Arkansas. Though he moved away, we still kept in touch.

Both of these men — Tom and Sonny — were very different men, yet each taught me something of what it means to be a man. Tom helped me laugh and develop my vivid imagination. Sonny taught me to love the woods, showing me how to hunt and be respectful of wildlife, and he taught me to be tough.

Both of these men sacrificed their time to be mentors and father figures in my life, and because of their sacrifice, I came to see that being a man was not nearly as intimidating as I had made it out to be. I learned that I didn't have to be afraid of other men. I learned that I didn't have to be afraid of becoming a man myself. These men shaped who I am today. Learning to laugh at Tom's jokes helped me relax and brought me a sense of belonging. Hunting with Sonny gave me the confidence to go after something and accomplish it, a confidence that later helped me get through high school and college. Both of these men helped me to become the man I am today.

They helped rewrite the story of my life.

CHAPTER 10

OF MUSTH CYCLES
AND MENTORING

It's better to build boys than mend men.
Truett Cathy, founder of Chick-fil-A

I FIRST MET DONALD MILLER at a Thai restaurant in Sellwood, a quaint, artsy area of Southeast Portland. Don has a big laugh that fills up the room. And he is disarmingly sincere, just like in his books. Several of us were having dinner with Don to talk about an audacious dream—starting a movement that would potentially transform the lives of the fatherless generation. As we finished our curry chicken and Pad Thai, we began exploring our vision.

Don had recently seen a documentary about orphaned African elephants, and he shared the story with us. The documentary followed the plight of twenty-five orphaned male elephants that were just entering adolescence; in other words, these were "teenagers." For elephants, this stage of adolescence is known as the "musth cycle," which is marked by heightened aggression and green pus that runs down their hind legs. Because these particular elephants were fatherless, they had perpetual musth cycles. They were unable to move beyond this phase of development, and some of the teenage "boys" were starting to cause trouble. They were tearing up the reservation and killing other animals. They were renegades without direction.

Don described one incident where rogue elephants took out their aggression on a few rhinos bathing in the local mud pool. An elephant walked up next to a rhino and without any warning speared it with its tusks and held it underwater until it drowned. According to Don, these elephants were not acting like normal elephants. Lacking a father in their lives, they had no way of knowing what was "appropriate" behavior for an elephant.

Sometimes two of the rogue elephants would clash in a violent and bloody fight. In his book *To Own a Dragon*, Don explains:

> When both beasts, bloodied, lumbered their separate ways alone—without a family, without a tribe—I couldn't help but identify. I have never killed a rhino, or much of anything for that matter, but there have been times in my life when I didn't know exactly how to be. I mean, there were feelings, sometimes anger, sometimes depression, sometimes raging lust, and I was never sure what any of it was about. I just felt like killing somebody, or sleeping with some girl, or decking a guy in a bar, and I didn't know what to do with any of these feelings. Life was a confusing series of emotions rubbing against events. I wasn't sure how to manage myself, how to talk to a woman, how to build a career, how to—well, be a man.[38]

Understanding the role of older elephants proved helpful in solving the problem of these rogue teenage elephants. Scientists went out and found older elephants from other tribes. Many of these elephants were fathers, and some were old enough to have fathered several generations of elephants. After the scientists introduced the elders to the rogue teenagers, they observed an amazing change. Immediately, the teenagers calmed down, and their musth cycles ended within a few days. The presence of these older elephants changed something, socially and biochemically, that brought an end to their destructive wildness. All that was required was the presence of older father figures — older elephants that could rub shoulders with them, give them guidance, and accept them into the tribe.

This story became the catalyst for what would become The Mentoring Project. And our small group that sat around the table eating Thai food formed the core of our organization. The Mentoring Project now exists as a nonprofit organization to inspire and equip the church to create sustainable mentoring communities. Every day, we're honored to see men coming alongside the fatherless, walking beside them, and showing them their place in the tribe.

THE MENTORING PROJECT

We believe that the faith community has the people and the resources to reach this generation. Most of the churches we work with simply need the right tools. Some of them need a compelling vision that leads to action.

Several years before I joined this organization, I had worked on a similar movement that was addressing the growing need for fatherless ministry. My dream was to start a movement that would restore hope to this fatherless generation, so in 2002, I began writing a doctoral dissertation on this topic of fatherlessness and created a blog and a website. My life story was slowly turning into a life mission.

Then Don called me to talk about The Mentoring Project and invited me to help steer this growing movement. We recognized that change requires vision, and vision must be reinforced by achievable goals. Our starting vision at The Mentoring Project is to equip and support one thousand churches, which will mobilize ten thousand men and inspire them to become mentors to this fatherless generation of boys.*

> Our starting vision is to equip and support one thousand churches, which will mobilize ten thousand men and inspire them to become mentors to this fatherless generation of boys.

We believe that the key to real and lasting change is activating churches and inspiring them with God's heart for this ministry. We are trying to beat this drum as loudly as we can, and we are praying for ten thousand men who will rise up to be heroes and fathers. We know that even if we reach our goal, it will still fall short of our ultimate hope—a mentor for every fatherless boy—but hey, it's a start. *It's something.*

• • •

The more I work with mentors, think about mentoring, and see mentoring happen, the more I understand that mentoring is more about relationships than about programs. Clearly, organization and plans are necessary for anything to succeed, but our programs have to be measured by the quality of relationships they serve and sustain.

We define *mentoring* as "an intentional relationship with the goal of seeing the mentee grow and mature into a complete adult." We look for men who can fill the role of the older elephants as they walk alongside a boy, giving him guidance, teaching him to understand what his strength is for, showing him how to work, how to relate to women, and how to contribute to the larger community.

---

* Find out more at *www.thementoringproject.org.*

MENTORING AS REDEEMING THE STORY

Statistics have shown that one-to-one mentoring is the most effective way to reach a fatherless child. Children with mentors are 46 percent less likely to do drugs, 33 percent less likely to resort to violence, 53 percent less likely to drop out of school, and 59 percent more likely to improve their grades. One-to-one mentoring has also been shown to lower the rates of teen pregnancy, suicide, and gang involvement in communities.[39]

Mentoring tells a child that he is cared for, that he matters, and that he is not alone. Mentoring shows a child how to be respectful and how to interact with peers and elders. Mentoring gives a child confidence in his talents, gifts, and natural abilities, which helps shape his pursuits, education, and eventual occupation.

> One-to-one mentoring is the most effective way to reach a fatherless child.

Many counselors agree that healthy and loving human relationships are the most powerful behavior modifier in the world. Fatherless children lack these loving relationships and often feel lonely, flawed, and incomplete. It is in relationships where the fatherless generation has been wounded the most deeply. Thus, it is in relationships where reconciliation must begin.

• • •

One of our best friends is a woman named Elizabeth. Nearly fifteen years ago, Elizabeth began spending time with a young girl, Annie, whom she met through Big Brothers and Big Sisters. At the time, Annie lived at home with her mom and younger brother. Her dad was absent. Their house was filthy, filled with dog and cat excrement. The house smelled like a Dumpster.

Annie's mom kept the television blaring loudly at all hours of the day, and she used blankets to cover the windows, so the house was always dark. Because of the filth and chaos in the house, Annie slept outside on the back porch. No one seemed to care that she had no place in the house.

During her time in school, Annie's dream was to be a Girl Scout. Her mom had been setting aside money for several months to save for a uniform. But when the VCR broke, the Girl Scout money was used to purchase a new VCR. Annie never became a Girl Scout.

Annie's little brother was frequently disruptive at school, screaming at teachers and students, threatening to kill anyone who disagreed with him. Whenever her brother would explode in fits of rage, Annie was the only one who could calm him down. The teachers and school counselors eventually stopped calling Annie's mom to help them with her son and called Annie instead.

Annie once took a dime and convinced a nursery owner to sell her a couple of iris bulbs, which she planted for her mother. Her counselor later said that her ability to see beauty in the world was her method of surviving. Her school counselor said that Annie was someone who was able to see beauty in the darkest places. Annie would spend hours looking at the clouds in the sky or staring at the trees. She was always looking for beauty, insisting that others see it too. She drank beauty in long, deep draughts. It replenished her. It reminded her of bright places — places other than the hole in which she lived.

Then Annie met Elizabeth.

Annie was quiet at first. Not used to the attention. Not used to having anyone notice her. But after several years together, their relationship developed to a point where Annie asked if she could move into the house with Elizabeth's family. Annie fit right in. Her new brothers and sisters immediately bonded with her and treated her like she belonged.

Soon after, Elizabeth enrolled her in a Christian group that was similar to the Girl Scouts. At one of the first meetings, the group was reading the Bible and came across Proverbs 31, a chapter about a wise woman who takes care of her house and family. Annie was blown away by what she read. She couldn't believe there were really women like this, women caring for their homes and families. But Annie thought about Elizabeth. Elizabeth modeled many of the same qualities of the Proverbs 31 woman. Before long, Annie started calling Elizabeth "Mom."

> Mentoring is the garden in which healthy and organic relationships grow.

In the years that followed, Elizabeth and her husband spent a great deal of time with Annie, building a reservoir of love and trust. They worked hard to show her that her past was not her future and that she did not have to live the rest of her life as a victim. Before long, Annie came to know the love and the unmerited grace of Jesus.

Elizabeth recalls a time, soon after this, when Annie called to Elizabeth. Annie was standing by the light switch, and the dimmer was turned all the way down. It was dark in the room. "This is what my life was like before I found Jesus," she said to Elizabeth. Then Annie started to slowly turn up the dimmer: "This is what my life is like since I found Jesus, and it's getting brighter and brighter."

Today, Annie is an entirely different person. The beauty that Annie looked for in nature now lives in her. As a result of being around Elizabeth and her family, that beauty began to bloom. Annie is always smiling, and she shines like a bright light, a bulb without a lamp shade. Annie is a hard worker, and she has conviction and character. She is fully embraced by her new family and recently served as the maid of honor at Elizabeth's daughter's wedding.

• • •

As the story of Annie and Elizabeth illustrates, intentional mentoring can literally change lives — forever. But its harvest is usually a slow one. It takes time. It takes consistent and faithful presence. To borrow a phrase from author Eugene Peterson, mentoring is not so much a sprint as "a long obedience in the same direction."

Mentoring is the garden in which healthy and organic relationships grow. It produces fruit that leads children to do better in school, with their peers, at home, and in life. These relationships are the grounding roots that solidify and help set their future growth and direction. Mentoring is the soil in which young lives bloom — through a process one of our TMP mentors, Bil, calls "beautification."

CHAPTER 11

ANATOMY OF A MENTOR

We must not shield ourselves from the reality of the situation if we expect to speak a healing word to the next generation. We can hardly expect postmoderns to take seriously our good news that God can be their Father if we are unwilling to enter their fatherlessness with the same intimacy with which Christ entered our world in the Incarnation.

"Because Fathers Matter," Critique magazine

IN JUNE 2009, I was honored to attend a presidential town hall meeting at the White House to participate in the Task Force for Fatherhood and Healthy Families conversation. This was part of President Obama's initiative to highlight the importance of fathers and community mentors.

During the trip, I shared my story with Judy, the former president of the Big Brothers and Big Sisters organization. I thanked her for her service and told her about my Big Brothers, Tom and Sonny. At the town hall meeting were dozens of other men and women who were doing unsung and heroic things for our country.

I was honored to meet Etan Thomas, who plays basketball for the NBA's Washington Wizards. Etan is nearly seven feet tall with huge dreadlocks. He is bright and articulate and is a featured writer on blogs and news columns. Etan regularly goes into D.C.-area juvenile detention centers and prisons to conduct writing workshops with a group called Free Minds Book Club and Writing Workshop.

The first thing he does when he speaks to a group is to ask the young men how many of them had a father. In crowds ranging from fifty to one hundred, usually only a couple of boys raise their hands. This gives him insight into his audience and opens the door to speak to the boys from a more personal place. Etan then teaches the boys how to write and express themselves. He told me that he is always shocked by the amount of pain that comes out during these sessions.

After the town hall meeting, I was walking from the White House, trying to find the meeting place for the Task Force on Fatherhood and Healthy Families. As I made my way, I ran into Carey Casey, another member of the task force.

Carey is a class act. He carries himself like an international ambassador. He is humble, genuine, and articulate. Carey served as a chaplain for the Dallas Cowboys under Coach Tom Landry and as a pastor at Lawndale Community Church in inner-city Chicago. He is currently the chief executive officer of the National Center for Fathering (*www.Fathers.com*). Carey recently wrote a book called *Championship Fathering*,* and while we were walking, he explained the message of his book and his organization. He has set a number of benchmarks that he communicates with the men he speaks to so that they can have a solid framework for measuring success.

---

* Carey Casey, *Championship Fathering: How to Win at Being a Dad* (Colorado Springs: Focus on the Family Publishing, 2009).

As we talked, Carey shared three fatherhood benchmarks that serve as simple handles men can grasp: *loving*, *modeling*, and *coaching*. I quickly realized that these same benchmarks for successful fathering also apply to mentoring, and so these now form the basic training outline for our mentors at The Mentoring Project.

BENCHMARKS FOR EFFECTIVE MENTORING

Benchmark #1: Loving. As a mentor, love is most clearly demonstrated, particularly early in the relationship, through unconditional and consistent presence. One of the most significant things a mentor does is simply show up, time after time.

Willie is one of our mentors, and for the past few years, he has faithfully met with a fatherless boy named Lehzan. I was talking with Willie at a baseball game and asked him about the development of their relationship. Once a week, Willie checks in with Lehzan's teachers to track how he is doing at school. He also has an open line of communication with Lehzan's mother. Sometimes Willie has to teach Lehzan how to deal with the hardships in life. "When something is going on at school," Willie says, "it always comes back to what is going on at home. And I'm not sure there are many others in Lehzan's life who are able to enter into both worlds and be an unconditional and consistent presence."

Lehzan's mother admits he has dramatically changed since Willie has been in his life. But Willie is the first to say this change has not happened overnight. It has been a slow and sometimes comical process. Willie's first attempts at conversation with Lehzan were met with one-word responses. "Yes." "Fine." "Uh-huh." Sometimes Willie just got a blank stare. It took him a year of faithfully showing up before Lehzan finally opened up. In many of those early conversations, Willie had to continue enduring one-word answers or grunts. Lehzan just didn't want to talk. Now Willie and Lehzan have meaningful two-way conversations.

Presence. Involvement. Consistency. These are the primary ways a mentor communicates love to a child. The first thing a mentor must be willing to commit to is *showing up*. Without consistent involvement, it is impossible for a relationship to develop patterns of trust and familiarity. And without consistency, the mentor just becomes one more person in the ever-revolving door of relationships. After consistently showing up, week after week, month after month, trust is born. Somewhere along the way, lines begin to blur, and a more organic relationship happens. Time spent together becomes less of a list of items to check off and more of a source of joy.

The types of activities that mentors and mentees do together can also be varied and different, geared in such a way as to match their interests and personalities. What matters is not *what* you do together as much as the fact that you are spending time together—just *being* in each other's lives. Playing in the park, throwing a baseball, going to a game, washing the car, going fishing, or playing guitar—all of these activities are secondary to the relationship itself. Some of my best mentoring moments were not big, elaborate events. They were just doing the everyday activities of life—going to the car wash, the bank, the grocery store. Doing the real "stuff" of life often provides the best setting for developing lasting relationships.

A consistent presence is only the first step. For love to be felt, it must also be *expressed*. Some of the best dads and mentors that I know are masters at expressing appreciation. They are sensitive to and aware of what is happening in the lives of their children and are just as quick to tell them about it, offering words of praise, such as *great job, awesome, cool, fantastic, super, wonderful,* and *I'm proud of you*. Some men find it hard to say these things and prefer to write them in a letter or email. Regardless of how you choose to express your love, the words you say matter. Even today, twenty-five years later, I still vividly remember many of the encouraging things my mentors said to me. The loving words of a mentor, according to Proverbs 18:21, have "the power of life and death."

Love is more than an emotion or spoken or written words; it is also an *action*. We can have the most loving intentions, thoughts, and feelings, but unless we actually do something about them, our love is never known. We may have a strong desire to be a part of our mentees' lives and even feel genuine love for them, but if we don't show up, our best intentions don't really matter.

Love gives without favoritism. My wife is a prime example. Children follow her around like she is the pied piper. Once, when we were on a mission trip at Calcutta Mercy Hospital in India, hundreds of kids followed her around, smiling at her. With each one vying for her precious attention, she still managed to smile at and greet each of them.

My wife regularly reminds me that children, like adults, need to be treated with dignity and respect. Whatever a child may be talking about, whether it is about dollhouses or GI Joe action figures, it's important to that child. My wife brings the same attentiveness to a discussion of the latest My Little Pony that she would bring to a job interview at Apple with Steve Jobs.

Unconditional love is described in 1 Corinthians 13, the famous "love chapter." Though this passage refers to our relationships in the body of Christ, the type of love described is the same love that is needed by this generation. It's the love that these children are looking for in so many places. The love that they need from mentors. One thing that helps me think about my responsibility as a mentor is to substitute the word *mentors* for the word *love* in this chapter:

Mentors are patient, mentors are kind. They do not envy, they do not boast, they are not proud. They are not rude, they are not self-seeking, they are not easily angered, they keep no record of wrongs. Mentors do not delight in evil but rejoice with the truth. They always protect, always trust, always hope, always persevere.

A mentor is willing to ask questions and patiently listen. James 1:19 reads, "Everyone should be quick to listen, slow to speak." Listening is an underrated gift. If a mother works several jobs, a fatherless child often lives in a lonely world with a good chance that he or she rarely talks to anyone. Listening communicates value to children and says, "Whatever you say to me matters. *You matter.*"

Another manifestation of love is *celebration*. Achievements and birthdays should be remembered, recognized, and celebrated. Many fatherless children are overlooked. Their achievements pass by unnoticed. They should be recognized and encouraged by a mentor. Some children never hear from their fathers, even on their birthdays. Author Henri Nouwen notes the importance of birthdays and why they are so significant:

> On our birthdays we celebrate being alive. On our birthdays people can say to us, "Thank you for being!" Birthday presents are signs of our families' and friends' joy that we are part of their lives. Little children often look forward to their birthdays for months. Their birthdays are their big days, when they are the center of attention and all their friends come to celebrate.
>
> We should never forget our birthdays or the birthdays of those who are close to us. Birthdays keep us childlike. They remind us that what is important is not what we do or accomplish, not what we have or who we know, but that we are, here and now.[40]

Benchmark #2: Modeling. A mentor should also model Christlikeness. Communication experts tell us that we actually retain about 5 percent of what we hear and 30 percent of what we see, but we remember nearly 75 percent of what we see *and* do. Children can regurgitate information—things they've heard in lectures, for example—but for the information to stick, they need to see it and, when they have the opportunity, to participate in the learning process. Regardless of what we might say, a child will remember more of what we *do*. Our legacy as mentors will be measured by what we did or did not do.

The apostle Paul famously said, "Be imitators of me, just as I also am of Christ" (1 Corinthians 11:1 NASB). This verse gets at one of the key ideas behind mentoring. A godly mentor needs to have a vertical relationship with God. A mentor doesn't need to have it all together, but he should be growing in his faith as he follows the one both he and the mentee are trying to emulate.

This is the foundational element of mentoring. We cannot show others something that we have not known or understood. We only model and show people who we are. Our vertical relationship with God is the foundation for our relationships with others. God is our source and the motivation behind our love, our example and model that we show to our mentee. We must be willing to be mentored by God if we wish to model our life after his and imitate his example.

Most modeling takes place when we aren't even aware it is happening. Young people will notice the smallest details of our lives, and they will often surprise us with the details they pick up. As the old adages go, "Most learning is caught rather than taught," and, "Your life is the loudest sermon you will ever preach." These may be clichés, but they are true nonetheless.

When I was serving as a youth pastor, I experienced this dynamic firsthand. Sometimes it was comical. It was also frightening to realize the level of influence I had in the lives of these kids. They would talk and act exactly like me. One time, when we were outside playing kickball, we were walking in a straight line heading out to the field. I decided to spit on the ground and see how many of the boys would do it after me. At least seven of the boys imitated me. I mentioned this to a friend, and the two of us tried an experiment. We'd roll our sleeves up or down, walk with a swagger, say certain words, or make bird noises whenever we kicked the ball. Without fail, almost everything we did was immediately imitated.

Another key component of modeling is learning to admit our mistakes, even apologizing when necessary. Our mentees look up to us and imitate our behavior, but they also need to see that we are honest about our shortcomings. Doing so creates trust and safety and helps a child get off the performance treadmill and learn that life takes tenacity and determination. By walking through failures together, we reveal something about ourselves and about grace.

Dr. Robert Coleman, affectionately known by his friends and family as "Clem," was one of my professors when I attended seminary in Chicago. He has been a distinguished professor of evangelism and discipleship in several major seminaries throughout the country and has written numerous books, including *The Master Plan of Evangelism.*

Clem is the best preacher I've ever heard. He bounces on his toes as he preaches, as if he is shadowboxing. Grinning from ear to ear, he speaks with intensity and infectious joy, as though he is looking through a secret portal directly into heaven. He is a Hall of Famer when it comes to being a coach. He does it naturally but intentionally, recognizing teachable moments and bringing the Word of God into conversations.

While attending seminary, I took all of Clem's classes and even joined his "advanced discipleship" group, which met on Tuesday mornings at six o'clock. Sometimes we met in his home; at other times we met on campus. We shared life together, prayed together, and memorized Scripture together. He made himself available, even calling us "his boys." Clem wasn't perfect, but he was a faithful model of the life he preached. I spent as much time with him as I could, in the office, at lunch, or over coffee, even riding with him to his speaking engagements. My wife and I were honored to have Clem preach at our wedding.

Clem burned a vision in the minds of "his boys" for what he called "the Great Commission lifestyle." He taught us that when you study Jesus' life, you find a brilliant coach who gathered a few men around him and poured his life into them, loving them, teaching them, and discipling them to be disciple makers themselves. Then he sent these men out to change the world.

Clem showed us that this is the way each of us are called to be engaged in the Great Commission of making disciples of all nations. There was one thing, though, that I especially remember from my time with Clem. He once told us that on the day when he stands before the Lord, before the judgment seat of Christ, the Lord will ask him this simple but pointed question: "Where are your men?" In other words, where are the men you poured your life into? Where are the men you coached and discipled while you were on earth?

I recently asked Clem how he saw mentoring fitting into the Great Commission, and this was his response: "The mentoring way is the way of Jesus. When Jesus walked on earth, he was a model, a mentor, and a teacher to those around him. He intentionally poured his life into his disciples, teaching them, training them, and then unleashing them on the world. And you know, John, the effects from his original group are still being felt today."

Benchmark #3: Coaching. Along with loving and modeling, a mentor must be an effective coach. In the mentoring relationship, effective coaching is usually done after a relational platform has been built. Unlike football or baseball coaches, mentors usually have to earn the right to be heard. This sacred right is typically granted on the back end of loving and modeling.

Coaching can involve working with a mentee at school, teaching him to read, learn a trade, or repair a car. Coaching can be about teaching simple life skills. Many fatherless boys feel inadequate because they don't know how to do some of the basic tasks of life. They feel intimidated by simple things like tying a fishing knot, doing a pushup, cooking a hamburger, changing a tire, or throwing a curveball.

Coaching is also a means of value construction. It involves teaching a boy that it's not good to laugh at bad jokes or respond to immaturity and to the manipulation of others. It entails setting appropriate boundaries and teaching a child to be always respectful. It is expressed as we help a child know what is appropriate. Many fatherless children may not know the difference between an "inside" voice and an "outside" voice. They may not understand that they cannot act the same way in a restaurant as they do on the playground. A coach gently but firmly shows them appropriate behavior for each setting.

A good coach teaches a child how to appropriately relate to other people, especially his elders. At the same time, they must also be sensitive to the shame and rejection that a fatherless boy may carry with him. Fatherless boys may be emotionally fragile. Or they may be distrusting of masculine authority. If a coach corrects a boy too strongly, it may do more harm than good. Corrections may need to be sandwiched between compliments and carried out with sensitivity to the unique history of each child.

A good coach will also build an appropriate relationship with the child's mother, respecting the role that she plays in his life. Ask her to fill in the details you may not be aware of—the areas in which a child is excelling, the activities he is involved in, and the kinds of things he talks about at home. Mentors should make sure that their input does not undermine the role of the mother; as much as possible, try to make sure your involvement complements the positive efforts she may be making in raising her child.

A mentor who is attentive will have plenty of opportunities for teachable moments. Jesus frequently used simple stories and everyday items such as mustard seeds, figs, wells, bread, and fish to communicate eternal principles. Perhaps there are simple stories from your life or items that belong to your child that can lead to teachable moments.

Some men find coaching to be the hardest part of mentoring. When a child does something or says something inappropriate, it is often easier to turn away, hold your tongue, and remain silent. But if we truly care for the person, we will confront him with the truth and use the opportunity to teach our child. Deuteronomy 6:7–9 talks about the responsibility of parents to coach and teach their children the truth of the Scriptures:

> Impress [these commandments] on your children. Talk about them when you sit at home and when you walk along the road, when you lie down and when you get up. Tie them as symbols on your hands and bind them on your foreheads. Write them on the doorframes of your houses and on your gates.

Though it primarily applies to parents and children, the same idea applies to mentors who work with fatherless children. This passage reminds us that we must not be afraid to talk about the Scriptures with a child, even encouraging us to talk about the truth in the daily moments of life. You may find it helpful to memorize passages or key verses of Scripture in preparation for your time with a child. One of my teachers used to say that "memorizing Scripture gives the Holy Spirit a vocabulary," and whenever you encounter a tough situation or engage in a difficult conversation, God can bring that Scripture to mind and use it to deliver a timely word.

• • •

The 2009 Oscar-nominated movie *The Blind Side* is based on the true story of a fatherless boy named Michael Oher. As a boy, Michael lived a nomadic existence, sleeping in foster homes, on the street, and in different houses in the projects in inner-city Memphis. Michael's story was originally told in the 2006 book written by Michael Lewis titled *The Blind Side: Evolution of a Game.*

As a young boy, "Big Mike" was forcibly removed from the care of his mother, a drug addict. From that point on, he spent his life shuffling along with no aspiration, simply surviving. He was essentially homeless, crashing on the floors of whatever project house he could find. One day, a man named "Big Tony," who was letting Mike sleep on his floor, took him across town to apply at Briarcrest Christian School.

Until that point, Mike had just been passed along from grade to grade. He had never learned how to read and had spent his class time staring at his books and dreaming of playing basketball and becoming the next Michael Jordan. Sean Tuohy, a forty-two-year-old business owner and father of two children at Briarcrest, saw Mike walking around the school and noticed he always wore the same clothes—cutoff jeans and an oversized T-shirt. Sean later saw him at a basketball game and realized that Mike looked hungry. So he approached him and asked him what he had eaten for lunch. Mike's answer was unclear, and Sean realized that Mike probably wasn't eating much. The next day, Sean went to the Briarcrest office and set up an account for Michael Oher to have lunch.

A few weeks later, during Thanksgiving break, the Tuohy family was driving in the early morning on a cold and snowy day, when Mike stepped out from behind a bus. He was dressed in the same T-shirt and shorts that he always wore, and he was trying to keep warm. Sean pointed him out to his wife, Leigh Anne, and said,

"That kid I was telling you about — that's him. Big Mike."

"But he's wearing shorts," she said.

"Uh-huh. He always wears those."

"Sean, it's snowing!"

Leigh Anne insisted they pull over.

"Where are you going?" Sean asked.

"To basketball practice," Mike said.

"Michael, you don't have basketball practice," Sean said.

"I know," the boy said, "but they got heat there."

Sean didn't understand that one.

"It's nice and warm in that gym," the boy said.

That moment — when the Tuohys see Michael and turn the car around — is the moment of epic opportunity. It is the moment of decisive inbreaking, a divine moment when feelings and compassion are stirred into action. A moment that will end up changing all of their lives.

The next day Leigh Anne took Mike shopping for clothes. After having a hard time finding them in his size, she called Patrick Ramsey, a personal friend and the quarterback of the NFL's Washington Redskins. Leigh Anne wanted Patrick to see if any of the players had clothes that would fit the sixteen-year-old Mike. After a couple of days, Patrick called Leigh Anne and told her that no one on the Redskins wore clothes that big. He asked, "Just who is that kid?"

Mike lived with the Tuohys for several weeks until Leigh Anne eventually asked him if he would stay. She bought Mike a futon and a dresser to organize his clothes. Upon seeing the bed, Mike stared at it for a while and then said, "This is the first time I've ever had my own bed."

Sean and Leigh Anne worked steadily with Mike to raise his GPA from 0.6 to 2.6 at graduation. They spent countless hours with him, even hiring a personal tutor for him. After Mike graduated from high school, he was accepted into college, where he set out on an All-American football career. In the first round of the 2009 NFL draft he was picked by the Baltimore Ravens, and he started every game of his first season.

The impact the Tuohys had on Mike's life is immeasurable. Michael Oher went from being a homeless drifter living in the poorest part of the Memphis ghetto to a college graduate and an NFL star. The Tuohys insist that "God sent Michael to us." They simply answered the call.

There are scores of people answering the call all over North America. We need more people like that. People like Big Tony. People like Sean and Leigh Ann Tuohy. People like Clem. People like Etan Thomas. People who sacrificially give their lives to the fatherless. People who are changing the world, one relationship at a time.

CHAPTER 12

IN SEARCH OF A NAME

Bless me too, my father!
Esau, in Genesis 27:38

IN THE BBC REALITY SHOW *The Monastery*, an order of Benedictine monks opens the door of its abbey to five outsiders for an experiment in the monastic life. These five men were to live under the rule of Saint Benedict—silence, obedience, and humility—for forty days and forty nights. The goal was that each man would participate with the other monks in community and reflect on how their life together affected his identity and purpose.

The five men came from diverse religious, professional, and cultural backgrounds. Most were openly apprehensive about the experiment, the monastic tradition, and the existence of God in general. Some questioned God's gender and the ideal path to God, as well as if following God was a logical decision at all. They wondered how following God would impact their careers and decisions. One was a retired schoolteacher and an atheist. Another was a student at

Oxford and a spiritual seeker. Another was an emotional Irishman who had been involved with the IRA. His time at a Catholic monastery was both ironic and reconciliatory.

The men were asked to respect and follow the communal requirements. They, like the monks, were to observe silence at mealtimes, speaking only at Sunday lunch. They worked alongside the monks in their daily tasks in the garden and in the kitchen and were discouraged from using anything that would connect them to the outside world, such as televisions or cell phones. After only a few days of stillness — away from the relentless noise, hurry, and crowds — their hearts began to surface.

The Irishman wept openly, torn over the guilt of his past and the quest to find his identity in the present. Another man got hostile and defensive as he began to fend off questions about his openness to the monastic life.

Tony, a soft-core pornography producer, began struggling with questions about his vocation. Tony wanted to keep his job and his "life," but at the same time, he didn't want to lose what he was experiencing in the monastery. He began bringing his questions to his spiritual adviser, Brother Francis. With only two days left at the monastery, Tony shared his concerns with his mentor:

Tony: No, I am not going to give up my job. I am not going to go sit in a church all day and read the Bible and eat pot noodles. I need to live. I need my lifestyle. So I'm just a little bit worried. Part of me wants to keep the whole thing alive and carry it through. And I know that the minute I get out, it will fade.

Brother Francis: I want to give you something that I think will help with what you've just described. Over the last couple of weeks you have been talking about vocation. And I think this is very important. Vocation is about discovering who you really are and maybe what you should really be doing. And that is what we are trying to do here—discover who we really are.

I want to give you this stone, this white stone. We have our Christian name, our family name. But we also have another name, and it's called our "white stone name." And that comes from the book of Revelation [2:17], where the angel says, "Your new name is written on a white stone in heaven." I think our vocation is to find out what that name is, to find our white stone name.[41]

After Brother Francis shares with Tony, he places his hand on Tony's head and gives him a spoken blessing. Francis speaks words of peace and hope over Tony. Immediately after that exchange, we find Tony sitting outside in the dark, huddled up on a bench, deeply affected by the experience. Tony is in obvious anguish over the truth and power of what he has just felt.

I believe Brother Francis not only spoke into the life of Tony, the soft-core porn producer; he speaks to the heart of the father-less generation. These are the sons and daughters who don't know their true name. They are searching for who they really are. In their search, they bring this question of identity to anyone who will listen. They live with the overwhelming urge to pursue those who will affirm them and give them a name. They are willing to look anywhere to find it. A chemical fix. A gang. A video game buzz. An orgasm. A spouse. A baby.

> This generation is an Esau generation—a generation that has lost its birthright and is longing for the father's blessing. But the fathers of this generation can no longer bless them because they are gone.

This is not something most of them readily understand. Often they are so engulfed by the lostness of it all that they cannot *see*. All they can do is *feel* that they are broken. But they know that finding who they really are is part of their salvation. They know that in finding it, they have the hope of being found.

In many ways, fatherless sons and daughters are like Esau, crying out to his father, Isaac, over his lost blessing. Esau brought disdain on himself by selling his birthright, his place of responsibility and privilege in the family. And his relational heartbreak lives on in the hearts of the fatherless.

This generation is an Esau generation — a generation that has lost its birthright and is longing for the father's blessing. But the fathers of this generation can no longer bless them because they are gone. While this is a tragic reality, it is also a great *opportunity* to bring healing and reconciliation to a broken generation. When authentic relationships have been established, there are opportunities to speak words of blessing into the lives of those we mentor. These blessings directly affect the trajectory of young persons and can help them begin rewriting their stories of shame, rejection, and pain.

BESTOWING THE BLESSING

Throughout the Bible and in some cultures today, the father's blessing is a treasured and weighty gift. The father gives his blessing to his children, often reserving a special blessing for the firstborn. It serves as a "send-off," an empowering release that encourages a young man to rise up and take his place, contributing to the larger world. Authors Gary Smalley and John Trent tell us that a spoken blessing involves "meaningful touching" and "continues with a *spoken message* of *high value*, a message that pictures a *special future* for the individual being blessed, and one that is based on an *active commitment* to see the blessing come to pass."[42]

This blessing can be a life-changing experience for a fatherless child. Obviously, mentors need to use caution and wisdom to make sure that touch is always done in appropriate ways. At The Mentoring Project, we advise our mentors to err on the side of safety, giving a boy a high five or a fist bump. These simple acts can communicate worth to a

> The blessing casts a vision and serves as a rough blueprint, a life map that a person can step into with confidence and hope.

child. And for someone who lives with a constant sense of rejection and worthlessness, the communication of worth and value is invaluable.

The blessing also paints a special future for the one receiving it. This blessing takes into account the natural abilities and gifts of a child. It is important to affirm and praise the child for what he does and for who he is. In this way, it provides a foundation that anticipates God's design and plan for him without forcing him to follow a specific, preordained path.

It can be tempting for mentors (and parents for that matter) to "wish" a specific future for a child. Often, these hopes and dreams reveal more about us and what we want than the desires and gifts of the child. The blessing of a child affirms what we hope for him but also serves to "call out" and propel the child to move forward with confidence in his own unique gifting. The blessing casts a vision and serves as a rough blueprint, a life map that a person can step into with confidence and hope.

The blessing is given by a person who is actively committed to seeing it come to pass. While anyone can speak words, having an ongoing relationship built on trust gives power and authority to the words the child receives. In this sense, the blessing is a promise, similar to the one exchanged between the bride and groom that declares, "I believe in you. I look forward to our bright future together. And I am with you in this."

God used a man named Bill Smith to speak blessing into my life. I met Bill at a duck hunting club in Arkansas during my freshman year in college, and he stayed in touch with me for the next ten years. He was instrumental in shaping who I am today. Bill and I hunted together, memorized Scripture together, prayed together, and, in his words, "talked about romance and finance." Bill helped introduce me to the company of men. He called me and wrote me while I was in school in Chicago. I still have one of his letters. It reads:

> You are a man, and a good man, and a godly man with a great future. Just keep steady and on the course God leads you on, and you will realize his best!"

* * *

THE FATHER'S BLESSING

As he began his public ministry, Jesus came to the Jordan River to be baptized by John. In Matthew's account, John humbly objects to baptizing Jesus, knowing that he is unworthy to even untie Jesus' sandals. John baptized those who came as an outer symbol of an inner reality, the forgiveness of sins for which they had repented. John knew that Jesus had no need to repent or have his sins forgiven. Still, Jesus insisted on his own baptism, and after John baptized Jesus, we are told the Holy Spirit descended on Jesus like a dove, and a voice from heaven declared, "This is my Son, whom I love; with him I am well pleased" (Matthew 3:16–17).

In a moment rife with eternal significance, Jesus, the Son of the living God, was blessed by his Father. This was no accident or coincidence. The timing of this blessing came just before Jesus started his public ministry, which lasted three years and culminated in a brutal and triumphant death on a cross at a place called

> In the divine ordering of the life and ministry of Jesus, *position* came before *purpose*.

"The Skull." In the divine ordering of the life and ministry of Jesus, *position* came before *purpose*.

The timing of the blessing is also significant as we consider this event from the perspective of Luke. Luke tells us that following his baptism (3:21–22), Jesus is led by the Spirit into the desert, where he fasts for forty days and at the end of that time is tempted by Satan (Luke 4). In the wisdom of God's plan, Jesus receives this life-giving blessing as an encouragement to sustain him during the desert trials and temptations.

The temptations that Satan unveils in the desert directly target Jesus' relational position, his identity. They target who he is and what he is called to do. Two of the three temptations directly challenge Jesus' position by saying, "If you are the Son of God, prove it."

Satan could have chosen any number of ways to tempt Jesus, but he chose to focus on Jesus' identity as the Son, his divine relationship with the Father. Perhaps he understands that attacking the father-son relationship is the most effective way to destroy lives and force a lifetime of bitter bondage to resentment, shame, and unforgiveness. Satan knows that if he can fracture the foundational relationship between fathers and sons, he can use the resulting wound to bring a person — even an entire generation — to its knees, bowing in subjection before him, seeking to fill the emptiness that ensues.

We have a unique opportunity to speak words that shape the divine purpose and identity of a generation. When a mentor blesses his mentee, he lifts that person's head up and opens the window of his heart to show him Jesus. The spoken blessing of God—the idea that we can now belong to him because of Jesus—begins to heal the shame of fatherlessness and to reconcile a generation back to the Father.

> Our identity, our white stone name, is hidden with Christ in God.

Despite what an earthly human father does or does not say to a child, he must come to recognize that he is more than his father's son. Each of us, regardless of our past, was created for something bigger than any earthly purpose or relationship. Our identity, our white stone name, is hidden with Christ in God. Every fatherless person has a future bigger than being a victim to fatherlessness. Our destiny is found in the blessing that the Father gives to Jesus and to all who come to him: "This is my Son, whom I love; with him I am well pleased."

CHAPTER 13

SUSTAINABLE COMMUNITIES

As iron sharpens iron,
so one man sharpens another.

Proverbs 27:17

FOR SEVERAL YEARS, a group of my friends and I had a little party we affectionately called "Man Christmas." In many ways, it's just like any other Christmas party, minus the tacky sweaters, stockings, mistletoe, carols, holly wreaths, and gingerbread cookies. OK, it actually has very little to do with Christmas. But we do have presents. Man presents. Gear. Stuff like knives, boots, vintage cameras, and books about Johnny Cash.

What happens at Man Christmas stays at Man Christmas. Well, not really. It's really just several wannabe rednecks sitting around a table, snorting, eating, laughing, and bragging about how tough we are and how our wives think we're cooler than Elvis. Sometimes we wrestle or do something dangerous. We eat lots of red meat.

After dinner, we exchange presents. The unspoken rule is that these presents have to be testosterone packed, even if they are completely impractical. The greatness of a Man Christmas present is measured by how many grunts it receives. Some of the best ones are things like a used hammer or an indestructible flashlight. Food is good — like homemade deer jerky, cans of chili, or Tabasco sauce. One time, two of the guys built me a fully functional war hammer, just like the one Gimli the Dwarf uses.

After we exchange presents, we usually go outside and sit around a fire or a portable charcoal grill. We tell stories. Mostly they are the same stories every year, but we don't really care.

Every year, my friend Ben tells his frog-gigging story. Frog gigging is the practice of wading through waist-deep water late at night while wearing a headlamp and using a long pole with a miniature trident (spear) stuck on the end of it. The goal of frog gigging is to impale the hapless frogs and then fry them and eat their legs. On this particular night, as Ben tells the story, he was wading down a murky stream and felt a pull on the burlap bag tied to his waist. The bag, he tells us, was full of frogs. Apparently, a four-foot-long poisonous cottonmouth snake was pulling on the bag, trying to swallow a frog through the burlap. According to Ben, he nonchalantly lifted the bag out of the water with the snake still attached, calmly pulled out his Rambo knife, and whacked the giant snake in half, killing it with a single blow. Afterward, he wiped off the blade on his pants, spit, and kept on frog gigging. What *really* happened, we'll never know. Most of us think that Ben probably dropped the mostly empty bag into the water and ran back to his truck shrieking like a little girl.

I'm usually asked to tell the story about the time I got badly sunburned while fishing. I was outside all day long, and for some reason, I thought it was a good idea to take my shirt off. Later that night, I was as bright as a lobster. My skin was *en fuego*. I looked around frantically for some aloe vera but couldn't find any. Most of the stores were closed. So I found some shaving cream with aloe vera and slathered it all over my chest and back. When my roommate came home, he didn't know what had happened and couldn't figure out why I was covered in shaving cream. He thought it was hilarious. But to this day, it still makes perfect sense to me.

After we tell our stories, there comes a moment every year where we get really honest with each other. I have this massive claymore sword that we pass around, and whenever anyone has the sword, it's his turn to share. We talk about what our year had been like and what we hope to see happen in the next. We talk about our jobs or about losing our jobs, about our families and how we can be better husbands and dads. After we share, one of us prays. Then we sit there for a long time and stare at the fire.

Man Christmas has taught me that truth is beautifully communicated in the context of authentic community. I look forward to Man Christmas for months ahead of time. I look forward to laughing, eating, and sharing stories. But mainly I look forward to those moments when we get honest and real with one another and connect on a heart level.

We learn much about who we are through our experience of community with others. We learn from their stories, their experiences, and the lessons God is teaching them. We learn to love people and receive love from people in the context of community. There is something sacred about walking into a roomful of people who know you, love you, and accept you unconditionally.

Each of us naturally gravitates in the direction of community. God made us for community. And God loves us through community. He uses our community with one another to reveal his love to a lonely world. God loves us by accepting us into his family. He speaks directly to the shame of the fatherless and says, "You belong to me." God doesn't save us into isolation; he saves us into community. Sin separates us from God and from one another. Jesus restores us, unites us, and places us in community.

The early church understood this. They were fiercely devoted to one another. They met in homes and shared meals together. Whenever one of them was in need, others would quickly pitch in to help them out. The book of Acts tells us that many of these early believers sold their possessions and gave the money to anyone in need. It says they "were one in heart and mind" (Acts 4:32). None of them, we are told, "claimed that any of his possessions was his own, but they shared everything they had.... There were no needy persons among them. For from time to time those who owned lands or houses sold them, brought the money from the sales and put it at the apostles' feet, and it was distributed to anyone as he had need" (Acts 4:32–35).

> Truth is beautifully communicated in the context of authentic community.

The more I think about it, the more I understand that something else makes the Man Christmas bond so strong. At some point, most of us served together. Nick, Ben, and I used to lead a small group of high school guys called "the misfits." We poured our life into those guys and that ministry. We hung out, talked about life, played games. We read the Bible, prayed, studied, and shared life together. We loved and mentored these guys.

MENTORING IN COMMUNITY

Community is vital to mentoring. Mentors have a better chance of winning when they mentor together. Mentors who have a community are able to help one another and pray for one another. A mentoring community based in a church also provides stability for the children being mentored. If for some reason a mentor moves away or has to stop mentoring for any reason, a church community usually has a pool of potential mentors to draw from, and a child is not left without a mentor. Church communities promote mentor sustainability and commitment, which ultimately leads to better relationships.

Both mentors and mentees are encouraged in community with others. Children make new friends with other children being mentored, and they can observe how other mentors relate to their mentees. A mentoring community provides a safe and easy way for initial introductions to be made. Scheduling initial meetings between a child and a mentor in a group setting helps ensure that the introductions go smoothly. Mentor and child have an opportunity to get to know each other and take the initial steps toward building a relationship before spending time together in a one-on-one setting. Doing so often makes for an easier and more natural development of the relationship.

Mentoring in a group setting also takes some of the pressure off the mentor. They no longer have to plan every detail of the meeting. They can just show up and participate in the group activity. This provides helpful support to mentors, since it can be a challenge to come up with something new every week. Churches are natural conduits for these types of mentoring communities to grow and develop. Often, a faith community already has several planned events they offer on a weekly or monthly basis. They may already have an after-school program. These existing programs serve as doorway opportunities for a mentor to spend time with his mentee.

I recently met with a group of mostly retired men who have spent the last ten years together as part of a men's Bible study at a local church. These men are friends. They pray together, serve together, and joke with each other. They have a wonderful sense of community. Now, they are gearing up to mentor together at an elementary school in Southwest Portland. I sat down with them and shared a few thoughts about what it takes to be a mentor. These are men who had been blessed with a wonderful community of authentic relationships. Now they are becoming a blessing to a new generation. The strength of their fellowship will help them reach a fatherless generation as they make a huge difference in the lives of these children.

My friend Duke recently showed me a video that tracked the mentoring relationship between two men, Travis and Ron, who live in Little Rock. Ron became Travis's mentor when Travis was a little boy, and they began spending time together as part of an urban ministry called STEP (Serving to Equip People)—a group-based ministry that emphasizes mentoring done in community, often evolving into organic relationships.

For fifteen years, Ron and Travis played ball together, studied together, and grew together as friends. Over time, their relationship grew to the point where Travis asked Ron to be the best man in his wedding. On the video, their connection was obvious. The two men talked about their relationship:

Travis: Ron believed in me. He encouraged me. Whenever I was going through something, you know—if I was worried about a test or one of my relatives was sick or whatever—he was going through it with me.

Ron: Our relationship wasn't a thing where, "Hey, we're supposed to meet on this day, from this time to this time, and then I will see you next week." It became a deal where we were hanging out several days a week. I wanted to include him in everything I was doing.

Travis: We would go shoot baskets. We would just hang out. He would take me to the library if I was struggling with homework—with math or whatever.

I remember one Christmas when Ron showed up, and he had, like, Christmas gifts. You know, it was something I didn't expect—that he and his family went out and bought me gifts. It was clothes, socks, pants—stuff I really, really needed. After he gave me the gifts, he told me that he really loved me and how much he cared for me. And you know, I was fourteen years old, and that was the first time anyone had ever told me they loved me. So that really meant a lot to me.

Travis: I never thought when we began this that ten to fifteen years down the road Ron would be the best man at my wedding. I don't think that was the plan.

Ron: Some of the feelings I went through on the wedding day were feelings of pure joy, of being there by Travis's side. After seeing him grow up from the time he was just a small kid until this point, and all the memories of the times we had together, all the things he had persevered through, fought through—and to now see him reach this point where he met the girl of his dreams and was marrying her—I have never been happier for anyone in my life. It was one of the best days of my life.

CHAPTER 14

REDEEMING THE STORY

WHEN I BEGAN WRITING this book in 2003, I started to hear the fatherless story everywhere. I heard it in advertisements and movies, in songs and television shows. I began hearing it from thousands of individuals online—on blogs and MySpace. Everywhere I turned, people were talking about it, mourning over it, laughing at it, raging about it, hurting from it. I also saw that the fatherless story, for most people, was not ending well.

The effects of fatherlessness were deeper and more profound than broken hearts. Many of the young people I talked with were acting out their rejection and shame, often destroying their own lives and the lives of those around them. I was discovering many of the things I've shared with you in this book—fatherlessness is the looming shadow behind so many problems of our society. At a deeper level, fatherlessness impacts the way this generation understands and relates to God.

> Fatherlessness is the looming shadow behind so many problems of our society.

As I began to see this, I also began to feel a passion, a growing sense that something—anything—had to be done to fight against it. I started praying to God, "How can we reach this fatherless generation?"

There are many answers to this question. Many of the answers that people suggest today are preventative measures. We can help engaged couples better prepare for marriage. We can encourage and equip married couples to stay together as we point them to counseling, education, and support groups. We could do away with the idea of a no-fault divorce and move toward a more covenantal understanding of marriage. We could mandate that sperm banks no longer give sperm to single women, which ensures that a child is fatherless from the moment of conception. We could spend more of our resources on abstinence programs and talk with young men about how to honor and respect women, challenging them to be guardians of purity instead of thieves of it. We can call men to stay married to their wives—refusing to leave their families under any circumstance, till death do us part.

But as I prayed, wrote, and researched, I realized that as good as these answers were, none of them addressed the fatherless generation directly.

I also became more and more convinced that this was an issue God wanted the church to get involved in. After all, the church is called to imitate a faith that reflects the Father heart of God: "As God's chosen people, holy and dearly loved, clothe yourselves with compassion, kindness, humility, gentleness and patience" (Colossians 3:12). The church is called to administer compassion to the wounded children of each generation.

The church also has the largest army of volunteers in the world. Many of the greatest historical movements of compassion have been started and sustained by the church. Consider what a difference it would make if every one of the some 300,000 churches in the United States equipped and sent out an average of ten mentors? What kind of impact would that have?

I want to be clear: this is not just another program or the latest fad. I believe it is an issue that reflects the heart and character of God, who names himself the Father to the fatherless. There are almost forty verses of Scripture that are exclusively devoted to teaching us about God's heart for the fatherless. The Bible makes it clear that the God we serve is a Father, Defender, Protector, and Provider for the fatherless. If our God is the Father to the fatherless, how can we, who are called to be imitators of him, be any less?

I believe that God's answer to the question of how we will reach this fatherless generation has been answered. Since this is a generation that has been deeply wounded by the loss of a significant relationship, we must begin with the place of pain. It is in the healing of this relationship that future hope will be found. That's why I believe the most strategic way to reach this fatherless generation is through intentional, intergenerational mentoring.

> If our God is the Father to the fatherless, how can we, who are called to be imitators of him, be any less?

Mentoring is not just about showing charity and sympathy to troubled kids. Mentoring calls people to live incarnationally and requires people who are willing to sacrifice something to become the hands and feet of Jesus.

As I looked around, I found great examples of people who were rewriting the story of the fatherless. These were people who were doing heroic and sacrificial things to change what seemed to be inevitable and often tragic endings. Many of these heroes were single mothers and grandmothers—like my own—women who were shouldering both roles of parenthood as they provided for and nurtured their families.

Today, I see men like Carey Casey, who heads up the National Center for Fathering, training and providing resources to men so that they can be better dads. I see an inner-city church in Los Angeles that sponsors meetings with fatherless boys every Saturday, all day, in a group mentoring setting. They have been doing this faithfully and quietly for years, rewriting the story of hundreds of fatherless boys. I see a suburban church outside of Portland, Oregon, that has nearly fifty men mentoring boys whose fathers are in prison. I see "20/20 Vision for Schools," birthed and conceived by Jeremy Del Rio in New York, a dream to send thousands of Christians into public schools to mentor children, helping them learn to read and study better and to deal with life situations. I see STEP Ministries in inner-city Little Rock and my friend Joe White courageously leading a camp called Kids Across America outside of Branson, Missouri.

I also think of the work of Steve Warren, former defensive lineman for the University of Nebraska and the Green Bay Packers, who leads an organization called D.R.E.A.M. Steve works in several elementary schools to mentor youth. As we were talking about the importance of mentoring, Steve said, "What a great feeling to help impact someone's life in a positive way and help bring change. Our hope is to see the youth we work with graduate, further their education, give back, and become productive members in the community."

Every day, the mentors who reach out and love fatherless boys through The Mentoring Project inspire me and renew my spirit. These guys are changing destinies. I sense the swell of a growing movement. We are poised for a revolution. But it will take more. Much more. There are still millions of fatherless youth in our nation.

While I was visiting D.C., I remember standing inside the White House, amazed at the history that surrounded me and the meetings and conversations that had taken place there over the last centuries. I was encouraged that another conversation was taking place now. The president had recently called on the men of our country to step up and be better fathers. He took questions from the crowd and talked about his own experience of growing up fatherless and about the lasting imprint a father can make on the life of a child.

But that wasn't all. The president then called on men to be available to the youth of their larger communities and to serve as mentors to them:

> And we need dads, but also men who aren't dads, to make this kind of commitment not just in their own homes to their own families, but to the many young people out there who aren't lucky enough to have responsible adults in their lives. We need committed, compassionate men to serve as mentors and tutors, and Big Brothers and foster parents. Even if it's just for a couple hours a week of shooting hoops or helping with homework or just talking about what's going on in that young person's life. Even the smallest moments can end up having an enormous impact, a lasting impact on a child's life.

Perhaps my favorite part of that experience was when President Obama and Vice President Biden each spoke about their own experiences as fathers. They spoke with earnestness and conviction about how their children were more important than their positions as leaders of this country. They spoke about the joys of fatherhood, of spending time loving and being with their children.

Regardless of your politics, this is a call that every one of us can answer. It's a message that reflects the driving passion of my life and the mission of The Mentoring Project. And it's a message that reflects the heart of God. We are working and praying that God will continue to raise up committed mentors who are willing to have a meaningful and lasting impact on this generation.

MENTORING FOR LIFE CHANGE

Every child has great God-given potential — the potential to succeed, to create, to contribute, to build a family, and leave a positive legacy. Without the intervention of caring mentors, fatherless children often miss out on their God-given potential and become another negative statistic. Without caring mentors, the next generation is likely to make choices that will destroy their lives and forever change the future of our nation.

This is a moment of critical importance and tremendous opportunity. We believe it is a joy and a privilege to have this unique opportunity to serve fatherless children and their families. What if our churches looked inside their own walls and began reaching out to single mothers and their children? What if our churches became safe havens for fatherless boys? What if our churches become known throughout our local communities as places where fatherless boys and mothers can turn for guidance, mentoring, and support? How many lives could be changed?

I thank God for the men who have mentored me. Heroic men who sacrificed time and energy to make a difference in my life. We need men like this, men who will pour their lives tirelessly into the lives of others. Men who believe and live the words of Jesus: "It is more blessed to give than to receive" (Acts 20:35).

This is our moment. This is our opportunity to act courageously, to plant our feet firmly in the river of history. This is our chance to leave an eternal legacy, a legacy that is far bigger than our individual stories. But for us to act, we have to be fully present. We must open our eyes. We must see the midnight of this generation and fully recognize the darkness of the hour. We must see beyond the hopelessness of the midnight and anticipate the coming dawn.

The looming challenge of fatherlessness presents the church with an unparalleled opportunity. By the grace of God, we can redeem this story. We believe it can be rewritten so that there will be fewer suicides and teen pregnancies, less drug abuse, and fewer boys who end up in gangs and in our already full prisons.

We believe that mentors will be the quiet heroes in this movement, people like you who can guide this generation away from looming destruction and into the fullness of the life, community, and purpose we have in Jesus.

We believe you can make a difference.

JOINING THE MOVEMENT: THE MENTORING PROJECT

THE MENTORING PROJECT is responding to the American crisis of father-lessness by inspiring and equipping churches to mentor fatherless youth. We work in/with/through the local church to create sustain-able mentoring communities. We would be honored to explore part-nering with you and your local church to see this happen. At the same time, we are interested in starting "TMP City Conversations" in which we come alongside the local church at the citywide level.

There are three primary ways that you can join us at The Men-toring Project.

PRAY

We understand that "unless the Lord builds this house, we labor in vain." All great spiritual movements are birthed and fueled by prayer. Please pray for The Mentoring Project staff and board, our mentors and mentees, our vision, our decisions, our supporters, our partnerships, and for wisdom for the journey. Prayer is the most important way that anyone can serve us.

SERVE

Partner with us to reach this fatherless generation. Register your church on our website, follow the updates, and consider participating in what we are doing, by going through the training and creating a sustainable mentoring community. Pray about engaging other church leaders in your city with this vision.

GIVE

The Mentoring Project was started and has been sustained by generous people giving average monthly gifts of $10, $25, and $50. Some give more, some less. Every little bit helps. We would be honored to have your support of a monthly gift, knowing that your tax-deductible donation is changing lives.

Please go to *www.thementoringproject.org* and register your church to find out more and begin a conversation. We look forward to hearing from you and serving you in redeeming the story of this generation. The best is yet to be!

ACKNOWLEDGMENTS

I AM THANKFUL TO GOD for pursuing me and loving me even when I don't deserve it and never have.

I am thankful to my wife, Kari, for her many hours of reading and listening and believing. To my faithful mother and grandmother. To my dad: although we have lived in different states for most of our lives, I am really glad we are friends. To the many mentors who have helped me along the way: Bill Smith, Robert Coleman, Larry Bratvold, Jim Pringle, Gail Walker, Keith Kirk, Sonny Gault, Tom Reid, and others. I am thankful for the amazing folks at Zondervan, especially Ryan Pazdur and Chris Fann. Thanks for believing in me and in the unsolicited proposal that I emailed you. You guys are exceptional.

I am thankful for the mentors, the supporters, and the staff of The Mentoring Project. You are rewriting the story of a generation — JZ, Mel, Trev, Shawnte, Cat, Just Adams, Pastor Frazier, Ben, Jason, Don, Kurt, Shaun, Duncan, Jay, and the rest of the crew.

I am thankful to everyone who bought this book. I pray that it stirs and changes you.

NOTES

1. Cited in National Quality Improvement Center on Non-Resident Fathers, "Research on Father Absenteeism," *http://fatherhoodqic.org/research%20on%20 father%20absenteeism.shtml*. Of the 73.2 million children under 18 years old living in the United States in 2004, 27.9 percent (20.4 million) were living with a single parent (U.S. Census Bureau, 2005).

2. Robert S. McGee, *Father Hunger* (Ann Arbor, Mich.: Servant, 1993), 93.

3. Everclear, "Father of Mine," from the album *Best of Everclear* (Capitol Records, October 5, 2004).

4. Good Charlotte, "Hey Dad," from the album *The Young and the Hopeless* (Sony Records, September 2002).

5. P!nk, "Family Portrait," from the album *M!ssundaztood* (Arista Records, November 20, 2001).

6. Filter, "Take a Picture," from the album *Title of Record* (Warner Brothers, November 6, 1999).

7. Seth Godin, "Notice Me," *http://www.sethgodin.typepad.com/seths_blog/2009/10/ notice-me.html*.

8. Robert Bly, *Iron John* (1990; repr., Cambridge, Mass.: Perseus, 2004), 189, 198.

9. Frank Pittman, *Man Enough: Father's Sons and the Search for Masculinity* (New York: Berkley, 1993), xx.

10. Augusten Burroughs, *A Wolf at the Table* (New York: St. Martin's Press: 2008), 61–62.

11. Cited in "The Future: Set Adrift on a Sea of Fatherless Children," *Idaho Observer*, July 2003.

12. Cited in Fathers Unite, "Fatherless Homes Now Proven beyond Doubt Harmful to Children," *http://www.fathersunite.org/statistics_on_fatherlessnes.html*; Fathers for Life, "The Impact on Our Children," *http://fathersforlife.org/divorce/chldrndi-vstats.htm*; see also Patrick Fagan and Kirk Johnson, "Marriage: The Safest Place for Women and Children," *http://www.heritage.org/Research/Family/BG1535.cfm*.

13. Excerpt from *Fight Club* (20th Century Fox, October 15, 1999).

14. David Blankenhorn, *Fatherless America: Confronting Our Most Urgent Social Problem* (New York: HarperCollins, 1995), 1.

15. Daniel Patrick Moynihan, "A Family Policy for the Nation," *America* 113 (September 18, 1965): 283.

16. Quoted in Institute for American Values, "Marriage Breakdown Costs Taxpayers at Least $112 Billion a Year" (April 15, 2008), *http://www.americanvalues.org/coff/ pressrelease.pdf*.

17. Cited in Megan Bear, "Early Parental Loss a Risk Factor for Adult Psychiatric Illness," *http://www.meganbear.org/fatherlessstats.htm*.

18. Gordon Dalbey, *Healing the Masculine Soul: How God Restores Men to Real Manhood* (Nashville: Nelson, 2003), 142–43.

19. Quoted in Michael Reagan, *Twice Adopted* (Nashville: Broadman and Holman, 2004), 80–81.

20. Cited in Thomas McAdam, "Execution Date Set for Serial Killer John A. Muhammad," *Louisville City Hall Examiner* (September 20, 2009), *http://www.examiner.com/x-3747-Louisville-City-Hall-Examiner-y2009m9d20-Execution-date-set-for-serial-killer-John-A-Muhammad.*

21. David Blankenhorn, *Fatherless America: Confronting Our Most Urgent Social Problem* (New York: HarperCollins, 1995), 95.

22. S. L. Price, "The Revenge of Jeremy Shockey," *Sports Illustrated*, July 28, 2003, *http://sportsillustrated.cnn.com/vault/article/magazine/MAG1029212/index.htm,* July 28, 2003.

23. Excerpt from *Crips and Bloods: Made in America* (New Video Group, May 19, 2009).

24. Ibid.

25. Earl Paysinger, in a speech at Hispanic pastors' prayer breakfast (June 19, 2004, Radisson Hotel, Los Angeles).

26. Kelly Clarkson, "Because of You," from the album *Breakaway* (RCA Records, November 30, 2004).

27. Kathleen Kingsbury, "Pregnancy Boom at Gloucester High," *Time*, June 18, 2008, *http://www.time.com/time/world/article/0,8599,1815845,00.html.*

28. Kathleen Parker, "An Illegitimate Culture," *National Review Online*, June 27, 2008, *http://article.nationalreview.com/361842/an-illegitimate-culture/kathleen-parker.*

29. See Guttmacher Institute, "Facts on American Teens' Sexual and Reproductive Health" (January 2010), *http://www.guttmacher.org/pubs/FB-ATSRH.html;* Fathermag.com, "Fatherless Homes Statistics," *http://www.fathermag.com/news/2756-suicide.shtml;* Decisions, Choices, and Options, "Facts on Fatherless Homes," *http://www.decisionschoicesandoptions.org/fathers.html.*

30. See March of Dimes, "Fact Sheet: Teenage Pregnancy" (November 2009), *http://www.marchofdimes.com/professionals/14332_1159.asp.*

31. From a conversation with Kelly Clarkson (June 11, 2009).

32. Monique Robinson, *Longing for Daddy* (Colorado Springs: WaterBrook, 2004), 5

33. Cited in Separated Parenting Access & Resource Center, "Divorce and Fatherhood Statistics," *http://deltabravo.net/custody/stats.php.*

34. Donald Miller, *Blue Like Jazz* (Nashville: Nelson, 2003), 1.

35. Paul Vitz, *Faith of the Fatherless: The Psychology of Atheism* (Dallas: Spence, 2000).

36. A. W. Tozer, *The Pursuit of God* (Harrisburg, Pa.: Christian Publications, 1948), 16.

37. Excerpt from a letter written by Matt Redman (October 1, 2009).

38. Donald Miller, *To Own a Dragon: Reflections on Growing Up without a Father* (Colorado Springs: NavPress, 2006), 32–33.

39. Cited in Jane Quinn, "Where Need Meets Opportunity: Youth Development Programs for Early Teens," *The Future of Children* (Fall 1999), 111–12.

40. Henri Nouwen, *Bread for the Journey: A Daybook for Wisdom and Faith* (New York: HarperCollins, 2006), 20.

41. Dialogue from *The Monastery*, BBC documentary (May 10, 2005).

42. Gary Smalley and John Trent, *The Blessing* (1986; rev. ed., Nashville: Nelson, 2004), 30.

CPSIA information can be obtained
at www.ICGtesting.com
Printed in the USA
LVOW13s1526090317
526326LV00001BC/1/P